THE ART

I

II

THE ART OF PROPHESYING

With

THE CALLING OF THE MINISTRY

William Perkins

THE BANNER OF TRUTH TRUST

THE BANNER OF TRUTH TRUST
3 Murrayfield Road, Edinburgh EH12 6EL
P.O. Box 621, Carlisle, Pennsylvania 17013, USA

*

The Art of Prophesying first published in Latin 1592
and in English 1606
The Calling of the Ministry first published 1605
First Banner of Truth revised edition 1996
ISBN 0 85151 689 0

*

*

Typeset in 10¹/₂/12pt Plantin
at The Banner of Truth Trust, Edinburgh
Printed and bound in Great Britain
by BPC Paperbacks Ltd
A member of the British Printing Company Ltd

Contents

Foreword

Christians throughout the world today owe a considerable but largely unrecognised debt to the great Puritan preacher and theologian William Perkins.

The bare facts of Perkins' life are these: born in 1558 in Marston Jabbet in Warwickshire, he received his formal education at Christ's College, Cambridge. He graduated B.A. in 1581, but remained at Christ's as a fellow until 1595; he served as lecturer (preacher) in the church of Great St Andrews from 1584 until his death in 1602 at the age of forty-four.

A man of considerable ability Perkins has been described as 'the Puritan theologian of Tudor times'.[1] Deeply committed to the awakening and transforming of professing Christians, he recognised the central importance of Christian godliness and the strategic, God-given significance of what transpired in the pulpits of England. With this vision he laboured to proclaim the gospel. Abundant testimony to the power with which he did this now fills the three great folio volumes of his *Works*.

Perkins stands out in the post-Reformation history of the church in England because of the enormous impact his preaching made on generations of preachers of the gospel. Something of his burden to see a genuinely biblical and powerful ministry can still be felt in the treatises

---

[1] M. M. Knappen, *Tudor Puritanism* (Chicago, 1939), p.375.

here republished. While somewhat modernised, they come in virtually unabbreviated garb.

Concern for the advance of the gospel was not always the leading feature of William Perkins' life. He was far from Christ in his early days at Cambridge. But in the mercy of God, like the prodigal son, he 'came to himself'. According to tradition this awakening began when he overheard a woman threatening her son, 'Hold your tongue, or I will give you to drunken Perkins yonder.' Doubtless various influences played their God-ordained roles, including perhaps his tutor, the remarkable evangelical preacher Laurence Chaderton. In any event, wonderfully drawn to Christ, Perkins now laid his whole life before his new Master in gratitude and tribute, and began to preach, first of all to condemned prisoners in the castle jail. Later he would exercise his considerable gifts from the pulpit of Great St Andrews, where he continued to minister until his death.

Such was the impact of Perkins' ministry that when the young John Cotton heard the church bell tolling for his death he rejoiced that his conscience would no longer be smitten by the preacher's sermons. A decade later when the twelve-year-old Thomas Goodwin came up to Cambridge in 1613, 'the town was then filled with the discourse of the power of Mr Perkins his ministry, still fresh in men's memories'.

Perkins' preaching was marked by the so-called 'Plain Style'. The description is self-explanatory: in sharp contrast to 'witty' preaching which employed the fashions and devices of human eloquence and classical rhetoric, Perkins believed preaching should conform to the apostolic touchstone of being 'the open manifestation of the truth' (*2 Cor.* 4:2). A new 'spiritual' model for preaching thus arose which could be traced back to the examples of the great biblical prophets such as Moses, Elijah, Isaiah,

Jeremiah, John the Baptist, and, yes, Paul and the Lord Jesus Christ himself. In exemplifying this model, Perkins' pulpit ministry was characterised by biblical exposition marked by great 'plainness of speech' (2 *Cor.* 3:12). Unfolding and applying the text of Scripture in a straightforward and simple, yet vigorous and direct style of speech and manner were its hallmarks.

Not that the plain style was lacking in wit or in the powerful use of the imagination; but the employment of these was always aimed at the mind in order to affect the conscience, and not merely to impress and delight aesthetic taste by clever oratory or a display of education and learning. In the plain style, spiritual taste was everything; only those who possessed it appreciated the 'pure spiritual milk' of biblical teaching.

Illustrative of this is the experience of Robert Bolton (1572–1631) a student of Lincoln and Brasenose Colleges at Oxford. On a visit to Cambridge this proud breaker of the commandments heard Perkins preach and thought he was 'a barren empty fellow, and a passing mean scholar'. But then God took hold of him and brought him through deep and painful conviction of sin, and this same Bolton came to believe that Perkins was 'as learned and godly a divine as our church hath for many years enjoyed in so young a man'.

The form of the plain style was as follows: the preaching portion, be it text or passage, was explained in its context; the doctrine, or central teaching of the passage was expounded clearly and concisely; and then careful application to the hearers followed in further explanation of the 'uses'. Thus the message of the Scriptures was brought home in personal and practical, as well as congregational and national applications to the hearers. What does Scripture teach? How does this apply to us today? What are we to do in response? How does Scripture teach us to do it? These became the issues handled with seriousness and vigour in the pulpit. Biblical and classical erudition was frequently present, but usually veiled; the sermons of many plain-style preachers scintillated with vivid language and illuminating illustration; but the main business was to preach Christ and to reach the heart. Everything was subservient to this.

Thus the plain style was more than just a formula for biblical exposition; it was marked by a further apostolic credential: power. At its centre lay a searching examination of and appeal to the consciences of those who heard the exposition of the meaning of Scripture.

Perkins believed that preaching should 'rip up the hearts' of those who heard it; but by the same token he saw the preacher as a spiritual apothecary whose knowledge of biblical remedies enabled him to bathe the wounds and heal the spiritual sicknesses of God's people with the grace of Christ. As the pages that follow demonstrate clearly, Perkins realised that the application of God's word must be made to a wide variety of spiritual conditions. Like his spiritual heirs the Westminster divines, he recognised that this was possibly the most demanding aspect of preaching, but also potentially the most significant.

In his preaching at Great St Andrews, Perkins proved to be an outstanding example of the principles he enunciated, and he set the standards which such pulpit giants as John Cotton, Thomas Goodwin, John Preston, Richard Sibbes and many others would emulate. It is this rich personal dimension that breathes a spirit of authenticity into these pages. Although they come to the reader somewhat transformed from the language of the sixteenth century into that of the twentieth century, the ring of truth about them cannot be missed.

Presented here are Perkins' outstanding tracts, *The Art*

of Prophesying and *The Calling of the Ministry.* Common to these works is a driving concern to see God's glory honoured and his word given its true place in the life of the church.

The Art of Prophesying
The Art of Prophesying was first published in Latin in 1592 and was translated into English in 1606, four years after Perkins' death.

The title alone is likely to attract purchasers in the contemporary church scene and it may therefore be necessary to explain exactly what Perkins means.

As a glance through the chapters immediately indicates, for Perkins prophesying is the task of the minister of the gospel as he stands in the great succession of biblical prophets and apostles who expounded God's word and prayerfully stood between God and the people:

> There are two parts to prophecy: preaching the Word and public prayer. For the prophet has only two duties. One is preaching the Word and the other is praying to God in the name of the people.[1]

For this role the *sine qua non* is a clear understanding of the message of Scripture and an ability to explain and apply it to the people. Perkins therefore sets out to provide a survey of the nature and contents of Scripture, and of the principles by which we may rightly handle and interpret it. He does this with simplicity, charm and no small practical insight into personal study of the Bible. While not providing a complete system of biblical interpretation, he supplies us with a little handbook of instruction which will still be found valuable today by

---

[1] See p. 7 below.

those who need to review their approach to Bible study and by many who are just beginning it.

But as one might expect from Perkins, the distinctive element in *The Art of Prophesying* is the attention he gives to the *application* of Scripture and the use of it in public preaching. Here he provides instruction, stimulus and challenge for all who handle God's word in public, whether in leading group Bible studies, teaching children and young people, or preaching in larger gatherings of God's people.

Unlike many other manuals which provide only principles of literary interpretation (sometimes giving no hint of any difference between the Bible and secular literature), the starting place for Perkins' work is rooted in the New Testament's teaching that Scripture is useful for doctrine, reproof, correction and training in righteousness (*2 Tim.* 3:16). In his view the task of understanding God's word is not complete until the purpose for which it has been given (its 'usefulness') has been grasped.

As is widely recognised today, one of the major educational influences on William Perkins was the new logic associated with the name of the Frenchman, Pierre de la Ramée (1515–1572). It emerged in Cambridge in large measure through lectures which Perkins' tutor Laurence Chaderton gave on Ramée's work. The modern reader will catch the flavour of this new method by noting the way in which Perkins uses a two-fold division as he explains and analyses the nature of preaching. Prophecy as such consists of two parts, (i) preaching and (ii) praying. Preaching can be analysed into (i) preparation and (ii) proclamation. Preparation involves (i) interpretation and (ii) division. Division includes (i) partition and (ii) application.

Whatever one makes of the influence of this new

Ramist logic as a tool for understanding and explaining preaching, no one should be able to read *The Art of Prophesying* prayerfully without catching an echo of the heartbeat of the great spiritual movement in which Perkins played such a strategic role. This is a work which will not only stimulate further, more accurate and deeper meditation on God's word; it should also stir up within us stronger desires to have God's word applied to our lives.

The Calling of the Ministry

The two parts of this work, first published in 1605, similarly bring us into the crucible of the reformation of the church. These addresses, taken down by Perkins' disciple William Crashaw, expound Job 33:23–34 and Isaiah 6 and direct our attention to what God calls ministers of the gospel to do and to be.

It is a general rule that as it goes with the pulpit so it goes with the people. There is, therefore, a special timeliness for us today in this tract, when there seems to be a lack of clarity in so many quarters about the *duty* of ministers. Certainly there is little *dignity* accorded to their role in the world.

A ministerial friend recalls that while he was mowing his lawn one day two small boys arrested him with a question in order to settle an argument between them. Said one, 'Mr ——, you are the *prime* minister, aren't you?' That the Christian ministry should be confused with the dignity of high political office is so unlikely today that this may strike us as amusing. In the secular world the work of the gospel ministry is set at a discount and in many cases publicly despised or at least caricatured. The tragedy is that to a certain extent this has also become true within the church. One evidence of it, common to Perkins' time and ours, is the way many ministers of the gospel struggle to sustain themselves and their families and do what they can to finance their ministries on all too inadequate remuneration. Almost inevitably therefore ministers of the gospel can themselves feel that their office and their persons are demeaned.

This is the age in which we live. But in many respects this was also the age of Perkins. He saw the same trends we do: able Christians succeeding in the secular world and enjoying the comforts of excellent salaries and the respect that accompanies a good position while their friends in the Christian ministry enjoy relatively little in the way of comfort or respect. But Perkins had learned to think with a biblical mind and see with the eyes of faith, and ministers today must do the same. If the greatest privileges that can be bestowed on an individual in this world are the forgiveness of sins, justification and reconciliation with God, adoption into his family and the assurance of eternal glory – then there is no more highly privileged duty, no more dignified position in the world than that of the minister of the gospel who is given the task of opening the kingdom of God to those who believe.

Perkins goes to considerable lengths to stress this high privilege. Indeed he does so in ways that might easily touch the raw nerve endings of contemporary egalitarian, individualistic – and certainly of the self-help – views of the Christian life. He insists, for example, that it is the distinctive privilege of the minister of the gospel to pronounce the forgiveness of sins. That this should be regarded as 'priestcraft' is perhaps an indication of how little we today think of the ministry as a special and holy calling and as the means by which God chooses to make his word of grace known to us.

Having rejected the word of God, it is to family physicians, hard-pressed for time, to analysts and psychiatrists that men and women now turn for the exorcism of the

demons of the mind, and for the freeing of the conscience from the guilt that sears it. Others turn to the pop
counsels of the day for assurance that their lives will be
'OK'. These occupations command respect and a following by contrast with the gospel ministry. But sedatives
and 'forgiving ourselves', or our family, or society are no
substitute for being told that God has forgiven us. Since
it is *against God* that we have sinned (*Psa.* 51:4), he alone
can forgive us. It is to the gospel of Christ that we must
go to have our consciences cleansed, and therefore to the
minister of that gospel sent to us by Christ for our good.
Grasp this, be we pastor or church member, and we will
begin to understand how great the duties and dignities of
the ministry of the gospel really are.

In these pages William Perkins' words come in the
updated clothing of more modern English. But more
than modernised language is required if his work is to
bear fruit today. The lasting principles of what he says
need to be translated into flesh and blood terms in our
pulpits and in our lives. It is one thing to admire the art
of preaching and to understand the duties and dignities
of the ministry; it is another thing to labour and pray that
what we admire in Perkins' teaching will be illustrated in
the ministry of the gospel in our own day. But under God
the reading of these pages written so long ago by William
Perkins will serve to drive us in the right direction.

SINCLAIR B. FERGUSON
Westminster Theological Seminary
Philadelphia, U.S.A.

*The publishers wish to express their appreciation to Kelvin Pritchard
for providing the electronic copy of these works of Perkins and thus
prompting the modernised version of these valuable treatises.*

THE ART OF PROPHESYING

Preface

The pages which follow have been written for faithful ministers of the gospel and for all who are concerned about and pursue the knowledge of holy learning.

The preparation of sermons is an everyday task in the church, but it is still a tremendous responsibility and by no means easy. In fact it is doubtful if there is a more difficult challenge in the theological disciplines than that of homiletics. Its subject matter is prophecy, which is a 'higher gift' indeed (cf. *1 Cor.* 12:31), whether we think about its dignity or its usefulness.

The dignity of the gift of preaching is like that of a lady helped into and carried along in a chariot, while other gifts of speech and learning stand by like maidservants, conscious of her superiority.

In keeping with this dignity, preaching has a twofold value: (1) It is instrumental in gathering the church and bringing together all of the elect; (2) It drives away the wolves from the folds of the Lord. Preaching is the *flexanima,* the allurer of the soul, by which our self-willed minds are subdued and changed from an ungodly and pagan life-style to a life of Christian faith and repentance. It is also the weapon which has shaken the foundations of ancient heresies, and also, more recently cut to pieces the sinews of the Antichrist. So, if anyone asks which spiritual gift is the 'most excellent', undoubtedly the prize must be given to prophesying.

The better something is, the more it deserves to be carefully presented with a wide variety of rich and wise counsel. But this everyday task is frequently described in a scarcely adequate and even impoverished manner by comparison with the attention other disciplines receive. I have, therefore, carefully studied the writings of the theologians, composed a series of rules and principles from their teaching, and tried to explain them in a way that will be both useful and easily remembered.

I am now committing these reflections on preaching to print – to be approved if they have any value, to be criticised and rejected if they have any inadequacies. If you are persuaded of this style of preaching, walk on with me; if you have some doubts, inquire with me; if you begin to see points at which you have wandered, come back on to the right path with me; if you see that I have strayed, call me back to the road you are on. Your appreciation of me will become disapproval soon enough if you do not like godly and moderate-minded men! But if anyone has petty complaints about these pages – few as they are – my conscience is a strong enough defence against all criticism, because my only concern has been to serve the church of God. So I commit you to him, and this little book on the art of prophesying to you as well as to him.

WILLIAM PERKINS
12 December 1592

Introduction

The study of prophesying involves a commitment of the mind to acquire the ability to exercise prophecy rightly. Prophecy (or prophesying) is a solemn public utterance by the prophet, related to the worship of God and the salvation of our neighbours, as the following passages indicate: 'But he who prophesies speaks edification and exhortation and comfort to men' (*1 Cor.* 14:3). 'But if all prophesy, and an unbeliever or an uninformed person comes in, he is convinced by all, he is convicted by all' (*1 Cor.* 14:24). 'For God is my witness, whom I serve with my spirit in the gospel of His Son' (*Rom.* 1:9).

1. *The Art of Prophecy*

There are two parts to prophecy: preaching the Word and public prayer. For the prophet (that is, the minister of the Word) has only two duties. One is preaching the Word, and the other is praying to God in the name of the people: 'Having . . . prophecy, let us prophesy in proportion to our faith' (*Rom.* 12:6); 'Restore the man's wife, for he is a prophet, and he will pray for you and you shall live' (*Gen.* 20:7). Notice that in Scripture the word 'prophecy' is used of prayer as well as of preaching: 'The sons of Asaph, of Heman, and of Jeduthun, who should prophesy with harps, stringed instruments, and cymbals' (*1 Chron.* 25:1); 'The prophets of Baal called on the name of Baal from morning even till noon . . . And when midday was past, they prophesied until the time of the offering of the evening sacrifice . . .' (*1 Kings* 18:26, 29). Thus every prophet's task is to speak partly as the voice of God (in preaching), and partly as the voice of the people (in praying): 'If you take out the precious from the vile, You shall be as My mouth' (*Jer.* 15:19); 'And Ezra blessed the Lord, the great God. Then all the people answered, "Amen, Amen!"' (*Neh.* 8:6).

Preaching the Word is prophesying in the name and on behalf of Christ. Through preaching those who hear are called into the state of grace, and preserved in it. God has 'given us the ministry of reconciliation . . . Now then, we are ambassadors for Christ, as though God were pleading through us; we implore you on Christ's behalf, be reconciled to God' (*2 Cor.* 5:18, 20); 'God from the beginning chose you for salvation, through sanctification by the Spirit, and belief in the truth, to which He called you by our gospel' (*2 Thess.* 2:13, 14); 'The gospel is the power of God to salvation for everyone who believes' (*Rom.* 1:16); 'Where there is no revelation the people cast off restraint' (*Prov.* 29:18); 'How then shall they call on Him in whom they have not believed? And how shall they believe in Him of whom they have not heard? And how shall they hear without a preacher?' (*Rom.* 10:14).

2. The Word of God

The Word of God alone is to be preached, in its perfection and inner consistency. Scripture is the exclusive subject of preaching, the only field in which the preacher is to labour. 'They have Moses and the prophets; let them hear them' (*Luke* 16:29); 'The scribes and the Pharisees sit in Moses' seat [that is, they teach the doctrine of Moses, which they confess]. Therefore whatever they tell you to observe, that observe and do' (*Matt.* 23:2–3).

The Word of God is God's wisdom revealing from heaven the truth which is according to godliness. 'But the wisdom, which is from above is first pure . . .' (*James* 3:17); 'Paul, a bondservant of God . . . according to . . . the acknowledgement of the truth which accords with godliness' (*Titus* 1:1). The exceptional qualities of the Word, both in its nature and its effects, evoke our admiration.

The Nature of Scripture
The excellency of the nature of Scripture can be described in terms of its perfection, or purity, or its eternity.

Its *perfection* consists either in its sufficiency or its purity. Its sufficiency is such that as the Word of God it is so complete that nothing may be either added to it or taken from it which belongs to its proper purpose: 'The law of the Lord is perfect, converting the soul' (*Psa.* 19:7); 'Whatever I command you, be careful to observe it; you shall not add to it, nor take away from it' (*Deut.* 12:32); 'For I testify to everyone who hears the words of the prophecy of this book: If anyone adds to these things, God will add to him the plagues that are written in this book; and if anyone takes away from the words of the book of this prophecy, God shall take away his part from the Book of Life, from the holy city, and from the things which are written in this book' (*Rev.* 22:18–19).

The *purity* of Scripture lies in the fact that it stands complete in itself, without either deceit or error: 'The words of the Lord are pure words, Like silver tried in a furnace of earth, Purified seven times' (*Psa.* 12:6).

The *eternity* of the Word is its quality of remaining inviolable. It cannot pass away until everything it commands has been fully accomplished (*Matt.* 5:18).

Effects of Scripture

The exceptional character of the influence of Scripture lies in two things:

1. Its power to penetrate into the spirit of man: 'For the word of God is living and powerful, and sharper than any two-edged sword, piercing even to the division of soul and spirit, and of joints and marrow, and is a discerner of the thoughts and intents of the heart' (*Heb.* 4:12).

2. Its ability to bind the conscience, that is, to constrain it before God either to excuse or accuse us of sin: 'There is one Lawgiver, who is able to save and to destroy' (*James* 4:12); 'The Lord is our Judge, The Lord is our Lawgiver, The Lord is our King; He will save us' (*Isa.* 33:22).

The Word of God is in the Holy Scriptures. The Scripture is the Word of God written in a language appropriate for the church by men who were immediately called to be the clerks or secretaries of the Holy Spirit: 'for prophecy never came by the will of man, but holy men of God spoke as they were moved by the Holy Spirit' (*2 Pet.* 1:21). We speak of it as *canonical* Scripture because it is, as it were, a canon, that is a rule or line used by a master workman, by the aid of which the truth is first discovered, and then examined: '. . . and as many as walk according to this rule' (*Gal.* 6:16). Consequently the supreme, final determination and judgment of all controversies in the church ought to be made by it.

The sum and substance of the message of the Bible can be summarised in an argument (or syllogism) such as this:

Major Premise: The true Messiah shall be both God and man, from the seed of David. He shall be born of his heavenly Father's bosom. He shall satisfy the law. He shall offer himself as a sacrifice for the sins of the faithful. He shall conquer death by dying and rising again. He shall ascend into heaven. In due time he shall return for judgment.

Minor Premise: Jesus of Nazareth, the son of Mary, meets all of these requirements.

Conclusion: Therefore Jesus is the true Messiah.

In this syllogism the major premise is the scope or principal burden of the writings of all the prophets. The minor premise is contained in the writings of the evangelists and apostles.

3. *The Contents of Scripture*

The Scriptures are divided into the Old and New Testaments. The Old Testament is the first part of Scripture. Written by the prophets in Hebrew (with some parts in Aramaic), it chiefly unfolds the 'old covenant' of works ('Moses and the prophets', *Luke* 16:29). 'And beginning at Moses and all the Prophets, He expounded to them in all the Scriptures the things concerning himself' (*Luke* 24:27). It is divided into sixty-six books which are either historical, doctrinal, or prophetic in nature.

THE OLD TESTAMENT

Historical Books
The historical books record stories of things which took place, which illustrate and confirm the doctrine which is expounded in other books: 'Now all these things happened to them as examples, and they were written for our admonition' (*1 Cor.* 10:11); 'For whatever things were written before were written for our learning' (*Rom.* 15:4). There are fifteen historical books:

1.   *Genesis* is a history of the creation, the fall, the first promise of salvation, and of the state of the church preserved and kept within the context of private families.

2.   *Exodus* is a history of the deliverance of the Israelites from the Egyptians. It describes the exodus, the giving of the law, and the tabernacle.

3. *Leviticus* records the regulations for ceremonial worship.

4. *Numbers* is a history of the people's military activity in the land of Canaan.

5. *Deuteronomy* is a commentary which repeats and explains the laws found in the previous books.

6. *Joshua* describes the entrance into and possession of the land of Canaan under Joshua.

7. *Judges* provides a history of the corrupt and hopeless condition of the church and commonwealth of Israel from the days of Joshua up to those of Eli.

8. *Ruth* gives an account of the marriages and posterity of Ruth.

9. *I and II Samuel* record events in the days of the priests Eli and Samuel, and during the reigns of Saul and David.

10. *I and II Kings* narrate what happened in the days of the kings of Israel and Judah.

11. *I and II Chronicles* contain a methodical history of the beginning, increase and ruin of the people of Israel, and help to trace and explain the lineage of Christ.

12. *Ezra* contains a history of the return of the people from captivity in Babylon, and of the beginning of the restoration of the city of Jerusalem.

13. *Nehemiah* describes the restoring of the city which as yet remained unfinished.

14. *Esther* is a history of the preservation of the Jewish church in Persia through the action of Esther.

15. *Job* is a history which traces the causes of his trials and his various conflicts, with their eventually happy outcome.

Doctrinal Books
The dogmatic or doctrinal books are those which teach and prescribe the doctrines of our theology. There are four of them in the Old Testament.

1. *Psalms* contains sacred songs suitable for every condition of the church and its individual members, composed to be sung with grace in the heart (*Col.* 3:16).

2. *Proverbs* serves as a handbook of Christian behaviour and teaches us about piety towards God, and justice towards our neighbour.

3. *Ecclesiastes* reveals the emptiness of all human pleasures to the extent that they are experienced apart from the fear of God.

4. *The Song of Songs* is an allegorical description of the relationship between Christ and the church in terms of the relationship between a bridegroom and his bride (or a husband and wife).

Prophetic Books

The prophetic books contain predictions, either of God's judgments on the sins of the people or of the deliverance of the church which would be finally completed at the coming of Christ. These predictions of the prophets are interspersed with calls to repentance. They almost always point to the consolation which would be found in Christ by those who repent.

It was characteristic of the prophets to help the memory and understanding of their hearers by recording summaries of sermons which they preached at much greater length: 'Moreover the Lord said to me, "Take a large scroll, and write on it with a man's pen"' (*Isa.* 8:1); 'Write the vision and make it plain on tablets, That he may run who reads it' (*Hab.* 2:2).

The prophetic books are usually described as 'Major' or 'Minor'. The 'Major' prophets record in detail the things that are foretold; these include the prophecies of *Isaiah, Jeremiah, Ezekiel* and *Daniel*. Included here too are *The Lamentations of Jeremiah* which express the misery of the Jews about the time of the death of Josiah. The

'Minor' prophets deal more briefly or in less detail with things that are foretold for the future, or at least with some of them. These are: *Hosea, Joel, Amos, Obadiah, Jonah, Micah, Nahum, Habakkuk, Zephaniah, Haggai, Zechariah* and *Malachi*.

So much, then, for the Old Testament.

THE NEW TESTAMENT

The New Testament is the second part of Scripture. Its contents were written in Greek by the apostles, or at least were approved by them (cf. 'built on the foundation of the apostles and prophets', *Eph.* 2:20). They plainly expound teaching on the new covenant. Peter approved the Gospel of Mark, at whose instigation and appointment it was written by John Mark, according to early church tradition. And John the Evangelist also approved the Gospel of Luke. The view reported by Eusebius that two places in Paul's letters (*2 Tim.* 2:8 and *Rom.* 2:16) suggest that he was the author of that Gospel carries little weight. In these verses Paul is not speaking of the gospel as a book, but of his whole ministry, since he adds, 'for which I suffer trouble as an evil doer, even to the point of chains' (*2 Tim.* 2:9).

The New Testament contains histories and letters.

Histories

1. The four Gospels of *Matthew, Mark, Luke* and *John* contain the narrative of the life, deeds and teaching which Christ showed to the world, from the time of his conception until his ascension into heaven. Of these four authors, two were hearers and eyewitnesses, so that

they were able to give greater assurance of the truth of the history.

The difference between the Gospels can be expressed as follows: Matthew gives a clear account of the doctrines which Christ delivered. Mark sets down the history briefly; although his Gospel is not an abridgement of Matthew's Gospel, as Jerome thought. He begins his account in a quite different way, and proceeds in a different order, dealing with some things more generally and also inter-weaving some new material. Luke aimed at providing an accurate history, and describes events in a certain order. John is almost completely dedicated to displaying the deity of Christ and the benefits which we derive from it.

Jerome distinguished the evangelists from one another by their different approaches. He says Matthew is like a man, because he begins with the manhood of Christ; Mark like a lion, because he begins with the preaching of John the Baptist, which was like the roaring of a lion. He compares Luke to an ox, because he begins with Zechariah the priest offering his sacrifice. He compares John to an eagle, because he soars to the heights, as it were, and begins with the deity of Christ.

2. *The Acts of the Apostles* is an orderly history recording the work of Peter and Paul particularly, and illustrating the governing of the early church (cf. *2 Tim.* 3:10).

3. *Revelation* is a prophetic history of the condition of the church from the age in which John the apostle lived until the end of the world.

Letters
As for the Letters, thirteen of them are from Paul and cover the following themes:

1. *Romans*: justification, sanctification, and the duties of the Christian life.

2. *I Corinthians*: reforming abuses in the church at Corinth.

3. *II Corinthians*: Paul's defence of himself and of his apostleship against his opponents.

4. *Galatians*: justification by faith without the works of the law.

5. *Ephesians*
6. *Philippians*
7. *Colossians* — confirm the churches in doctrine and in the
8. *I Thessalonians* — duties of the Christian life.
9. *II Thessalonians*

10. *I Timothy* — prescribe the form of
11. *II Timothy* — ordering the church aright.

12. *Titus*: ordering the church in Crete.

13. *Philemon*: the reception of the runaway slave Onesimus.

Hebrews deals with the person and offices of Christ and describes the character of the faith which produces fruit in good works.

James expounds the good works which are to accompany faith.

I and II Peter deal with sanctification and the works of new obedience.

I John expounds the signs of fellowship with God.

II John was written to 'the elect lady' about perseverance in the truth.

III John, addressed to Gaius, is about hospitality and constancy in the good.

Jude emphasises constancy in the faith against the influence of false prophets.

These, then, are the books which belong to the canonical Scriptures.

THE CANON OF SCRIPTURE

There is strong evidence to show that these books alone, and no others, constitute the Word of God. One kind of proof enables us to know this, the other gives expression to it. Of the former kind there is only one, namely the inward testimony of the Holy Spirit speaking in the Scriptures, not only telling an individual within his heart but also effectually persuading him that these books of the Scripture are the Word of God. 'My Spirit who is upon you, and My words which I have put in your mouth, shall not depart from your mouth . . . from this time and for evermore' (*Isa.* 59:21).

The way in which we are persuaded is as follows. The elect, having the Spirit of God, first of all discern the voice of Christ speaking in the Scriptures. Furthermore, they approve the voice which they discern; and what they approve they also believe. Finally, believing they are (as it were) sealed with the seal of the Spirit. 'In whom also, having believed, you were sealed with the Holy Spirit of promise' (*Eph.* 1:13).

The church can bear witness to the canon of Scripture, but it cannot inwardly persuade us of its authority. If that were so the voice of the church would have greater force than the voice of God, and the whole state of man's salvation would be dependent on men. What could be more miserable than that?

More than one objection has been raised against this view by the Roman Catholic Church:

Objection 1: The Scripture is the Word of God by itself, but it is not clear to us that this is so except through the judgment of the church.

Answer: (i) This is an irrelevant contrast. For the first part of it shows the manner in which the Scripture is the Word of God (i.e. by itself as breathed out by God); the latter part shows not *the manner how*, but the *person to whom* it is the Word of God.

(ii) The Scripture itself testifies to itself with the kind of testimony which is more certain than all human oaths. For we have the voice of the Holy Spirit speaking in the Scriptures, who also works in our hearts a full persuasion of their inspiration, when we are engaged in hearing, reading and meditating on them. We do not believe something because the church says it is to be believed; rather we believe it because what the church says has first of all been said by Scripture.

As a matter of fact the church cannot stand, or its existence be imagined, apart from faith; and faith does not exist apart from the Word. It alone is the rule or object of faith; not the judgment of mere men, even of the holiest men.

(iii) The person who doubts the Scriptures will also doubt the testimony of the church.

Objection 2: The church has a proper role to play in exercising its judgment in determining such matters. Thus the letter which was sent from the special council of apostles and elders in Jerusalem was phrased in these terms: 'it seemed good to the Holy Spirit, *and to us*' (*Acts* 15:28).

Answer: (i) The sovereign or supreme judgment in matters of faith is the prerogative of the Holy Spirit speaking in the Scriptures. The ministry of judgment (or a ministerial judgment) is given to the church only because she must judge according to the Scriptures. Because she does not always do this, she sometimes fails.

(ii) The apostles were present at the council which was held at Jerusalem. They were men whose authority was to be believed in and of itself. But the church's ministry no longer possesses that immediate authority.

Thus the proof of declaration or testimony which the church gives to Scripture does not demonstrate or persuade us that it is God's Word. It only testifies to it and in various ways approves the true canon. Nevertheless, this proof is multi-faceted:

First, there is the perpetual consent of the church to the Scriptures. This begins with believers in the Old Testament period: to them were committed 'the oracles of God' (*Rom.* 3:2). It continues in the New Testament and the church:

(a) From Christ and the apostles, who cited testimonies out of those books;

(b) From the Fathers: Origen, Melito of Sardis, Athanasius, Cyril, Cyprian, Rufinus, Hilary, Jerome, Epiphanius, Gregory, and so on.

(c) From the Councils of Nicea and Laodicea.

Secondly, there is the partial consent of the pagan thinkers and even enemies of the faith who say the very same things which are taught in Holy Scripture; men such as Homer, Plato, Josephus, Lactantius, Cicero, Virgil, Suetonius, Tacitus and Pliny can be included here.

Thirdly, there is the antiquity of the Word. It contains a record of human history since the beginning of the world. By contrast the oldest secular histories were not written before the time of Ezra and Nehemiah, who lived in the fifth century before Christ.

Fourthly, the origin of Scripture is confirmed by the fulfilment of such prophecies as the calling of the

Gentiles, of the Antichrist and of the apostasy of the Jews.

Fifthly, there is the substance of Scripture's teaching: the one true God, the true worship of God, and the truth that God is the Saviour.

Sixthly, the harmony of all the different parts of Scripture.

Seventhly, the remarkable way in which the Scriptures have been preserved through all the periods of peril and times of general revolt the church has experienced.

Eighthly, the effect of Scripture: it converts people, and even although it is completely contrary to their thinking and desires, it wins them to itself.

Ninthly, the simplicity of its words which are full of the majesty of God.

Lastly, the holy authors did not avoid recording their own corruption; yet Moses commends himself, saying that he was the meekest of all men. That he does *both* is a further argument for believing that these writers were led by the Holy Spirit. Christ, who is described in the Gospels, clearly claims to be the Son of God, and one with God the Father. He directs all God's glory to himself. If this claim had not been right and true, Christ would have felt the wrath of God as Adam and Herod did, when they sought to make themselves like God. But what, in fact, happened was that God revenged his death upon Herod and upon the Jews, and upon Pilate, and upon those emperors who persecuted the church.

These, then, are the tokens of the divine origin of Scripture. In the light of these considerations it is clear that the Book of Tobit, the Prayer of Manasseh, the Book of Judith, the Book of Baruch, the Epistle of Jeremiah, the additions to Daniel, the Third and Fourth Books of Ezra, the additions to the Book of Esther, I and II Maccabees, the Book of Wisdom, and Ecclesiasticus, are not to be reckoned part of the canon for the following reasons:[1]

1.   They were not written by the prophets.

2.   They were not written in Hebrew.[2]

3.   In the New Testament neither Christ nor the apostles appeal to the testimony of these books.

4.   They include false teaching which is contrary to the Scriptures.

[1]   These books from the Apocrypha were included in the canon of Scripture by the Roman Catholic Church.
[2]   Many apocryphal books were written in Hebrew or Aramaic, but were preserved or known only in Greek until recently.

4. The Interpretation of Scripture

Thus far we have discussed the object of preaching. There are two parts to it: the preparation of the sermon, and the preaching of it. Here our Lord's words are relevant: 'Then He said to them, "Therefore every scribe, which is instructed concerning the kingdom of heaven, is like a householder, who brings out of his treasure things new and old"' (*Matt.* 13:52).

PREPARATION

In preparation there must be careful private study. Various scriptures underline this: 'Till I come, give attention to reading, to exhortation, to doctrine' (*1 Tim.* 4:13); 'Of this salvation the prophets have inquired and searched carefully, who prophesied of the grace that would come to you' (*1 Pet.* 1:10); 'In the first year of his reign I, Daniel, understood by the books the number of the years' (*Dan.* 9:2). Concerning the study of divinity, the following advice should be followed.

First, fix clearly in your mind and memory the sum and substance of biblical doctrine, with its definitions, divisions and explanations.

Secondly, read the Scriptures in the following order. Using grammatical, rhetorical and logical analysis, and the relevant ancillary studies, read Paul's Letter to the Romans first of all. After that, the Gospel of John. These are the keys to the New Testament. Thereafter, the other books of the New Testament will be more easily understood.

When you have completed this, study the doctrinal books of the Old Testament, especially the Psalms; then the prophetic books, especially Isaiah. Lastly, the historical books, particularly Genesis. It is very likely that the apostles and evangelists read Isaiah and the Psalms a great deal, since no other books of the Old Testament are as frequently cited in the New Testament as these are (about sixty passages from both Isaiah and the Psalms).

Thirdly, we ought to get help from orthodox Christian writers, not only from modern times but also from the ancient church. For Satan raises old heresies from the dead in order to retard the restoration of the church which has begun in our own time. The Antitrinitarians have simply painted a new coat of varnish on the views of Arius and Sabellius. The Radical Anabaptists repeat the doctrines of the Essenes, Catharists, Enthusiasts, and Donatists. The Swenkfeldians revive the views of the Eutychians, Enthusiasts and others. Menno follows the Ebionites, and Roman Catholicism resembles the Pharisees, Encratites, Tatians and Pelagians. The Libertines repeat the views of the Gnostics and Carpocratians. Servetus has revived the heresies of Paul of Samosata, Arius, Eutyches, Marcion and Apollinarius. Lastly, schismatics who separate themselves from evangelical churches revive the opinions, facts and fashions attributed by Cyprian to Pupianus and of the Audians and Donatists.

We do not need to look for any novel way of rejecting and refuting these heresies; the ancient ones found in the Councils and the Fathers are well-tested and still reliable.

Fourthly, anything you come across in your studies that is important and worth noting should be recorded in tables or commonplace books, so that you have both old and new material at hand.

Fifthly, and most important of all, we must earnestly ask God in prayer to open our blind eyes to the meaning of the Scriptures: 'Open my eyes, that I may see wondrous things from Your law' (*Psa.* 119:18); 'I counsel you to buy from Me gold refined in the fire . . . and anoint your eyes with eye-salve, that you may see' (*Rev.* 3:18).

Commonplace Books
In connection with composing commonplace books, here is some practical advice:

1. Make a list of the most common headings of every point of doctrine.

2. Divide the right-hand pages of your book into columns, or equal sections lengthwise. Head each of these pages with a major topic, leaving the next page blank, so that extra space may be available.

3. Do not attempt to record everything you read in a book, but only things which are memorable or unusual. Do not write out quotes, but only the principal points with appropriate references. Make a note in the book itself too, so that you will be able to find the place referred to in your commonplace book.

4. Some things may be more difficult than others to catalogue accurately. You should therefore add an alphabetical table to help you relocate them easily.

5. Do not rely too much on your book. There is no point in writing things down unless they are carefully hidden in your memory too.

Preparation has two parts: the interpretation of the meaning of the passage, and the appropriate division of it for orderly exposition.

Interpretation

Interpretation is the opening up of the words and statements of Scripture in order to bring out its single, full and natural sense.

By contrast with this approach, the Church of Rome believes that passages of Scripture have four senses: the literal, the allegorical, the tropological and the anagogical. An illustration of this can be found in the way the figure of Melchizedek is understood. He offered bread and wine to Abraham (*Gen.* 14:18). The *literal* sense is that the king of Salem, with the food that he brought, refreshed the soldiers of Abraham, who were tired after their travel. The *allegorical* sense is that the priest offers up Christ in the mass. The *tropological* sense is that we are to give to the poor. The *anagogical* sense is that Christ who is in heaven shall be the bread of life to the faithful.

This pattern of the fourfold meaning of Scripture must be rejected and destroyed. Scripture has only one sense, the literal one. An allegory is only a different way of expressing the same meaning. The anagogy and tropology are ways of applying the sense of the passage.

The principal interpreter of Scripture is the Holy Spirit. The one who makes the law is the best and the highest interpreter of it. The supreme and absolute means for the interpretation is the Scripture itself: 'So they read distinctly from the book, in the Law of God; and they gave the sense, and helped them to understand the reading' (*Neh.* 8:8).

There are, however, three subordinate means to help us to interpret a passage of Scripture: the analogy of faith, the circumstances of the particular passage, and comparison with other passages.

The analogy of faith is a summary of the Scriptures,

drawn from its well-known and clear parts. There are two elements in it. The first is related to faith, which is handled in the Apostles' Creed.[1] The second concerns charity or love, which is expounded in the Ten Commandments. 'Hold fast the pattern of sound words which you have heard from me, in faith and love which are in Christ Jesus' (*2 Tim.* 1:13).

The circumstances of a passage can be clarified by the following simple questions: Who is speaking? To whom? On what occasion? At what time? In what place? For what end? What goes before? What follows?

A comparison of different passages involves comparing them with each other so that their meaning may be clearer. 'But Saul . . . confounded the Jews who dwelt in Damascus, proving [i.e. by comparing one thing with another] that this Jesus is the Christ' (*Acts* 9:22).

Comparing different passages may involve two things:

1.   The first involves comparing a statement in one context with the other places where it appears in Scripture. For example: 'Make the heart of this people dull, And their ears heavy, And shut their eyes; Lest they see with their eyes, And hear with their ears, And understand with their heart, And return and be healed' (*Isa.* 6:10). This is repeated six times in the New Testament (*Matt.* 13:14; *Mark* 4:12; *Luke* 8:10; *John* 12:40; *Acts* 28:27; *Rom.* 11:8).

When texts are repeated like this they often contain alterations for various reasons. Examples include:

[1] The Apostles' Creed was not written by the apostles, but forms of it appear from very early days of the church's life, and it has been viewed throughout the ages as a minimal summary of what Christians believe.

(i)   Exegetical: to clarify their exposition. Examples include:

>Psalm 78:2 cited in Matthew 13:35
>Psalm 78:24 cited in John 6:31
>Isaiah 28:16 cited in Romans 9:33
>Psalm 110:1 cited in 1 Corinthians 15:25
>Psalm 116:10 cited in 2 Corinthians 4:13
>Genesis 13:15 cited in Galatians 3:16.

(ii) Diacritical, to distinguish, indicate or clarify places, times and persons, as for example in the citation of Micah 5:2 in Matthew 2:6.

(iii) To limit the sense of a passage to the original intention and meaning of the Holy Spirit. Examples will be found in:

>Deuteronomy 6:13 in Matthew 4:10
>Isaiah 29:13 in Matthew 15:8
>Genesis 2:24 in Matthew 19:5
>Isaiah 59:20 in Romans 11:26.

(iv) For application, so that a type might be related to its fulfilment, the general to the special, and vice-versa. Examples include:

>Jonah 1:17 in Matthew 12:40
>Isaiah 61:1 in Luke 4:18
>Psalm 22.18 in John 19:28
>Exodus 12:46 in John 19:33
>Psalm 69:25 in Acts 1:20.

(v) For the sake of brevity, some things may be omitted. Omission may also occur because the words are not appropriate to the matter in hand. One example of this is the use of Zechariah 9:9 in Matthew 21:5.

2. The second kind of comparison involves comparing one context with another. Again these may be either similar or different. Places that are similar agree with one another in certain respects, perhaps in their phraseology and manner of speech, or in their sense.

Places that agree with respect to *phraseology* include:

> Genesis 28:12 and John 1:51
> Genesis 3:15 and Romans 16:20
> Genesis 8:21 and Ephesians 5:2.

Greek and Hebrew concordances prove very helpful for tracing examples of this kind.

Places which agree in *sense* are those which have the same meaning. Under this heading we should especially note the comparison of a general principle with a particular illustration of it. For example:

> Proverbs 28:13 and Psalm 32:3, 4
> 2 Samuel 15:25 and 1 Peter 5:6.

So much for places that are similar. Places that are unlike one another apparently do not agree with one another, either in phraseology or meaning. For example:

> Romans 3:28 and James 2:24
> 1 Kings 9:28 and 2 Chronicles 8:18
> Acts 7:14 and Genesis 46:27
> Acts 7:16 and Genesis 48:22
> Zechariah 11:13 and Matthew 27:9.

5. *Principles for Expounding Scripture*

The Scriptures are to be interpreted according to the nature of the passage which is being handled. These can be classified as either analogical and plain, or cryptic and dark.

Analogical places are those whose apparent meaning is clearly consistent with the analogy of faith. Here this rule is to be followed: If the natural meaning of the words agrees with the circumstances of the passage, then the natural meaning is the proper meaning. For example: 'To Him all the prophets witness that, through His name, whoever believes in Him will receive remission of sins' (*Acts* 10:43). The meaning of this text is quite clear, namely that Jesus Christ gives righteousness and ever-lasting life to those who believe in him. We can accept this interpretation immediately because it agrees with the analogy of faith, and with the Scriptures.

We ought further to realise that every article and doctrine which is related to faith and life and necessary for salvation is clearly stated in the Scriptures.

Cryptic or hidden passages are those which are difficult and obscure. For expounding them this rule and guide should be followed: If the natural meaning of the words obviously disagrees with either the analogy of faith or very clear parts of Scripture, then another meaning, one which agrees with both similar and different places, with the circumstances and words of the passage, and with the nature of what is being discussed, must be the right one.

An important example of this principle emerges in connection with interpreting the words, 'This is My body which is broken for you' (*1 Cor.* 11:24). Various interpretations have been given to this statement including: that the bread in the communion is actually the body of Christ, becoming so by conversion (the Roman Catholic view); or that the body of Christ is in, under, or with the bread (the Lutheran view). But to expound these words in either sense would be to disagree with a fundamental article of the faith: Christ 'ascended into heaven', and also with the nature of the sacrament, as a memorial of the absent body of Christ. Consequently another interpretation must be sought.

A different interpretation is that in this context the bread is a sign of the body. In this case the figure of speech known as metonymy is being employed – the name of one thing is used for something else which is related to it. This is an appropriate exposition for the following reasons:

First of all, it agrees with the analogy of faith in two ways:

1.   'He ascended into heaven'; he was taken up locally and visibly from the earth into heaven. Consequently his body is not to be received with the mouth at the communion, but by faith apprehending it in heaven.

2.   He was 'born of the virgin Mary'; Christ had a true and natural body which was long, broad, thick, and seated and circumscribed in one particular place. If this is so, the bread in the Supper cannot be his actual body but must be only a sign or pledge of it.

Secondly, this interpretation is consistent with the circumstances described in the passage (*1 Cor.* 11:23–26).

1. 'He took . . . He broke it.' It is hardly likely that Christ sitting among his disciples took and broke his own body with his hands! Bread must therefore be no more than a sign and seal.

2. '. . . broken [or given] for you.' The bread cannot be said to be given for us; the body of Christ was. Therefore the bread is not properly the body, but is so symbolically or as a sign.

3. 'The cup is the new covenant,' not literally but by metonymy. Since this is the case, there is no reason then why metonymy is not also used in the words, 'This is My body.'

4. Christ himself ate the bread, but he did not eat himself!

5. 'Do this in remembrance of Me.' These words assume that Christ is not corporeally present to the mouth, but spiritually present to the faith of the heart.

6. 'Till He comes.' These words assume that Christ is absent as to his body.

7. Christ did not speak about being under the form of bread, or in the bread; he said, 'This [that is 'this bread'] is My body.'

Thirdly, this interpretation is consistent with the nature of a sacrament, in which there must be an appropriate relationship and similarity between the sign and the thing signified. But that is impossible if the bread is literally the body.

Fourthly, this interpretation is consistent with other biblical usage (e.g. *Gen.* 17:10, 11; *1 Cor.* 10:4; *Rom.* 4:11; *Exod.* 12:11; *Acts* 22:16; *John* 6:35; *1 Cor.* 10:16).

Fifthly, it agrees with the laws of logic. Things which are essentially different (like bread and a body) cannot be identified in this way except by a figure of speech.

Sixthly, this interpretation fits in with everyday speech. In the ancient world, the fasces (the bundle of rods which were carried before Roman magistrates) were used as a symbol for government itself; the sceptre for the kingdom; the gown for peace; the laurel garland for triumph. To speak of the bread as the body of Christ is a similar figure of speech.

A number of important implications for interpreting the Scriptures follow from this rule of interpretation.

Implications

1. On occasion it is appropriate to supply words which are lacking in the text where this is consistent with the analogy of faith and with the circumstances and words of the context.

Examples of this can be found in Exodus 4:25, 19:4; 2 Samuel 21:16; Luke 13:9; 1 Corinthians 9:25.[1]

2. If an alternative explanation of the text involves changing one noun (or name) for another, this is an indication that a figure of speech is being employed. Some general principles for guidance may be helpful here:

(i) Anthropomorphism is a metaphorical use of language, in which what is appropriate for man is used in describing God. Thus, for example, the 'soul' of God indicates his life or essence. 'Shall not my soul be avenged on such a nation as this?' (*Jer.* 5:29, *Geneva Bible*). 'Head' denotes his superiority; 'the head of Christ is God' (*I Cor.* 11:3). God's 'face' refers to his favour or his anger; 'You hid Your face, and I was troubled' (*Psa.*

---

[1] In many Bible versions words supplied to make good sense of a statement are printed in italics. Perkins himself uses Ephesians 3:1 as an illustration, but it is doubtful if this is a correct reading of the text and it has been omitted here.

30:7); 'The face of the Lord is against those who do evil' (*Psa.* 34:16). References to his 'eyes' usually indicate his grace and providence: 'The eyes of the Lord are on the righteous' (*Psa.* 34:15). The 'apple of his eye' signifies something especially dear to him: 'he who touches you touches the apple of His eye' (*Zech.* 2:8). A reference to his ears normally indicates his hearing of our prayers. In a similar way, his nostrils represent his indignation, his hands stand for his power and protection, his arm for his strength and fortitude, his right hand for his supreme authority, his finger for virtue, his foot for government and might (e.g. in *Psa.* 110:1), his smelling for his accepting of something: 'and the Lord smelled a soothing aroma' (*Gen.* 8:21). Repentance is used for the change in things and actions which God executes.

(ii) Sacramental language, or more properly sacramental metonymy, involves the sign being used to denote what it signifies and vice-versa. Thus, for example, the tree of the knowledge of good and evil means the tree which is a sign of these. Similarly, circumcision is called both the covenant and the sign of the covenant (*Gen.* 17:10, 11). Abraham called the place on Mount Moriah where he was about to sacrifice Isaac when God stopped him (and the ram he found caught in a thicket was sacrificed instead) 'Jehovah-jireh' meaning 'The Lord will see or provide.' The place became a sign that the Lord would do so (*Gen.* 22:14). The stone which Jacob had used as a pillow the night he dreamed of the ladder which reached up into heaven is called Bethel, 'God's house' (*Gen.* 28:22). The sign is identified with what it signifies. Similarly the paschal lamb is the passing over (*Exod.* 12). The altar is called 'The Lord is my standard or banner' (*Exod.* 17:15). Jerusalem is named 'The Lord is there' (*Ezek.* 48:35). The priest 'makes atonement' (*Lev.* 16).

In the New Testament Christ is called a lamb: 'Behold! The Lamb of God who takes away the sin of the world!' (*John* 1:29). The paschal lamb is called Christ: 'For indeed Christ, our Passover, was sacrificed for us' (*1 Cor.* 5:7). In the same verse Christians are said to be 'unleavened'. Christ is called the propitiation (*hilastērion*) or the cover of the ark of the covenant (*Rom.* 3:25). Christians are said to be 'one bread' (*1 Cor.* 10:17); and the Rock is said to be Christ (10:4). In the same way baptism is the washing of the new birth (*Titus* 3:5); the cup is called 'the new testament', and the bread is said to be the body of Christ (*1 Cor.* 11:24–25). In such cases the sign is said to be the thing signified, but with the understanding that such language employs a figure of speech in which the sign stands for the reality it represents.

(iii) What is called the communication of the properties in Christ (when what is appropriate to his humanity is ascribed to his divine nature) is a synecdoche – the figure of speech in which the whole stands for the part, or vice-versa. Through the union of the divine and the human natures in the one divine person of Christ, what strictly speaking belongs to only one of his two natures is spoken of the whole person. Examples include: 'to shepherd the church of God which He purchased with His own blood' (*Acts* 20:28). 'No one has ascended to heaven but He who came down from heaven, that is, the Son of Man who is in heaven' (*John* 3:13). 'For had they known, they would not have crucified the Lord of glory' (*1 Cor.* 2:8). 'Jesus said to them, "Most assuredly, I say to you, before Abraham was, I AM"' (*John* 8:58). 'And Jesus increased in wisdom and stature, and in favour with God and men' (*Luke* 2:52).

This communication of properties applies only in the concrete, not in the abstract. By concrete I mean the whole person, as God, man, Christ; by abstract, either of the two natures considered as Godhead or manhood.

(iv) When something is said of God, which implies his involvement in evil, it must be understood as referring to his working permission. This is commonplace in the Old Testament 'And it yields much increase to the kings You have set over us, Because of our sins; Also they have dominion over our bodies and our cattle at their pleasure; And we are in great distress' (*Neh.* 9:37); 'The Lord has mingled a perverse spirit in her midst; And they have caused Egypt to err in all her work' (*Isa.* 19:14). God thus hardened the heart of Pharaoh (*Exod.* 11:10). Again, 'The Lord your God hardened his spirit and made his heart obstinate, that He might deliver him into your hand, as it is this day' (*Deut.* 2:30). 'For it was of the Lord to harden their hearts, that they should come against Israel in battle, that He might utterly destroy them, and that they might receive no mercy, but that He might destroy them' (*Josh.* 11:20); 'Nevertheless they did not heed the voice of their father, because the Lord desired to kill them' (*1 Sam.* 2:25). 'The destruction of Ahaziah came of God' (*2 Chron.* 22:7, *Geneva Bible*). 'He turned their heart to hate His people, to deal craftily with His servants' (*Psa.* 105:25). 'And if the prophet is induced to speak anything, I the Lord have induced that prophet, and I will stretch out My hand against him and destroy him from among My people Israel' (*Ezek.* 14:9).

But there are also examples of this in the New Testament: 'God gave them over to a debased mind' (*Rom.* 1:28). 'God will send them strong delusion, that they should believe the lie' (*2 Thess.* 2:11).

(v) Again, some things are described as if they were already finished. If in fact they are not yet finished, such statements indicate that they have already begun and are on the way to an anticipated fulfilment (e.g. *Gen.* 5:32, 11:26; *1 Kings* 6:2, 37; *Psa.* 119:8). In this way we can understand the kinds of statements made, for example, in Luke 1:6 and Philippians 3:12, 15.

(vi) Moral commandments or laws which mention a specific sin by name imply all sins of the same kind, including their causes and occasions, as well as whatever tempts us to them. They also command the opposite virtues. This is how Christ expounds moral laws in the Sermon on the Mount (see *Matt.* 5:21–48). John illustrates the same principle when he writes: 'Whoever hates his brother is a murderer' (*1 John* 3:15).

(vii) Threats and promises should normally be understood as implying certain conditions. Their outworking depends on whether or not faith and repentance are present in response to them. That is true particularly of some verses (although chastisement and the cross are exceptions to this rule, e.g. Ezekiel 33:14, 15; Jonah 3:4; Revelation 21:18). From what follows in the events themselves it becomes clear that the threat or promise was to be understood conditionally (e.g. *Jer.* 18:9, 10). Similar examples include Isaiah 38:1 and Genesis 20:3. Here, clearly, the outworking of God's will is involved, hence the distinction that was drawn by the scholastic theologians between the signifying will of God and the will of his good pleasure. By his *will of good pleasure* is meant that God wills something absolutely and simply without any conditions, such as the creation and governing of the world, or the sending of his Son. By his *signifying will* is meant that he wills some things with a view to some other thing, and as a condition of it. Because the condition annexed indicates the presence of God's will we are able to say that he does so will.

(viii) Superlative or exclusive speech used of one person of the Godhead does not exclude the other persons. It denies only creatures and false gods to which the true God, whether in one person or in more, is opposed. Thus Jesus calls the Father the only true God, but only to oppose him to all false gods (*John* 17:3). Further examples can be found in Mark 13:27, Romans 16:27; 1 Timothy 1:17. John 10:29 is an obvious example: 'My Father . . . is greater than all' does not mean greater than the other persons of the Trinity, but greater than all creatures. All the outward works of the Trinity, and all divine attributes are to be understood inclusively; they apply without exception to any of the persons.

(ix) When God is considered absolutely, or by himself, all three persons of the Trinity are meant. When the word 'God' is used along with another person of the Trinity, it denotes the Father (e.g. *2 Cor.* 13:13).

(x) A general word may have a particular meaning and vice-versa. Thus 'all' may mean 'many', and 'many' may mean 'all' (as Augustine made clear). We see this frequently in Scripture (e.g. *Gen.* 33:11; *Exod.* 9:6; *Deut.* 28:64; *1 Kings* 12:18; *Jer.* 8:6, 26:9; *Matt.* 4:23, 21:26; *John* 14:13; *1 Cor.* 6:12; *Phil.* 2:21). 'Nothing' may mean 'little' or 'small' (*John* 18:20; *Acts* 27:33). 'None' can be used for 'few' (*Jer.* 8:6; *1 Cor.* 2:8). 'Always' may mean 'often' or 'long' (*Prov.* 13:10; *Luke* 18:1, 24:53; *John* 18:29). 'Eternal' may mean 'a long time' if that suits the context best (*e.g. Gen.* 17:8; *Lev.* 25:46; *Deut.* 15:17; *1 Chron.* 15:2; *Isa.* 34:6; *Dan.* 2:4; *Jer.* 25:9). 'Everywhere' can mean 'here and there' (*Mark* 16:20; *Acts* 17:30). A negative is often limited in its significance to one particular matter (e.g. in *Psa.* 7:4; *John* 9:3). 'Not' may mean 'seldom', 'scarcely', or 'hardly' (*1 Kings* 15:5; *Luke* 2:37).

3.   The grammatical and rhetorical properties of words indicate their difference nuances of meaning:

Ellipsis (when one or more words are lacking) indicates brevity, or it may be an expression of deep emotion (*Gen.* 3:22, 11:4; *Exod.* 22:20, 23; *1 Chron.* 4:10; *Psa.* 6:3; *Acts* 5:39).

The exchange of the perfect tense, in which the past is used to express what will happen in the future indicates the certainty of what will happen (*Gen.* 20:3; *Isa.* 9:6, 21:9).

Pleonasm (repetition of a word or words), in the case of a simple repetition of the vocabulary, indicates: (i) Force and emphasis; the words signify more than their ordinary meaning (*Psa.* 133:2; *Luke* 6:46). (ii) A multitude (*Gen.* 32:16; *Joel* 3:14). (iii) Distribution (*Lev.* 17:3; *1 Chron.* 26:13; *2 Chron.* 19:5). (iv) Diversity and variety (*Psa.* 12:2; *Prov.* 20:10).

A different form of pleonasm occurs when one noun is governed by another. In the singular this is very significant and argues certainty (*Exod.* 31:15; *Mic.* 2:4). In the plural it signifies excellency as, for example, in Song of Songs; servant of servants (cf. also *Psa.* 136:2; *Eccles.* 1:2).

Pleonasm in the case of an adjective (sometimes also of a noun) signifies exaggeration or increase (*Exod.* 34:6; *Prov.* 6:10; *Isa.* 6:3; *Jer.* 7:4, 22:29, 24:3; *Ezek.* 21:28). In the case of a verb it either makes the speech more emphatic and significant, or else indicates and expresses vehemency, certainty, or speed (*Gen.* 2:7, 46:4; *Exod.* 13:17; *2 Sam.* 15:30; *2 Kings* 5:11, 8:10; *Psalms* 50:21, 109:10; *Prov.* 27:23; *Isa.* 6:9, 50:2, 55:2, 56:3; *Jer.* 12:16, 23:39).

Pleonasm in the case of a conjunction may indicate earnestness (*Ezek.* 13:10). A conjunction doubled increases the force of the denial (e.g. *Exod.* 14:11; *Matt.* 13:14).

Pleonasm in an entire sentence implies first, distribution (*Ezek.* 46:21); secondly, emphasis (*Exod.* 12:50; *Psalms* 124:1, 145:18); thirdly, the repetition of a sentence in different words is for elucidation (*2 Kings* 20:3; *Psa.* 6:9,10; *Isa.* 3:9; *John* 1:3).

All figures of speech are emphatic in function. They enlarge the sense of what is said. But in addition to giving literary and aesthetic pleasure they also serve to nourish faith, for example when Christ is put for the Christian, or for the church of God (*Matt.* 25:35; *Acts* 9:4). This certainly brings comfort to the faithful soul, and nourishes faith.

Irony (when what is meant is the opposite of what is actually said, sometimes in the context of mocking) often implies a rebuke for sin (*Judg.* 10:14; *1 Kings* 18:27, 22:15; *Mark* 7:9; *1 Cor.* 4:8).

Figures of speech which involve the *repetition* of a word or sound, are used for emphasis (*Psa.* 67:5, 6; *Isa.* 48:11; *John* 1:51). There is a remarkable example of this in Psalm 136 where repetition is used in every single verse.

A *question* may indicate various things: a strong affirmation (e.g. *Gen.* 4:7, 37:13; *Josh.* 1:9; *1 Kings* 20:27; *Mark* 12:24; *John* 4:35, 6:7, 10:13); a denial (e.g. *Gen.* 18:4; *Matt.* 12:26; *Rom.* 3:3); forbidding (*2 Sam.* 2:22; *Psa.* 79:10); the presence of emotions like admiration, compassion, complaining and fault-finding (*Psalms* 8:10, 22:1; *Isa.* 1:21. A concession indicates a denial and rebuke (as in *2 Cor.* 12:16, 17).

4. Apparent contradictions in Scripture can often be resolved by realising that the passages deal with different things although the vocabulary may be the same, or they may be dealing with different aspects, or perspectives or even different time-frames.

Examples of this include Psalm 7:8 ('Judge me . . . according to my righteousness') and Isaiah 64:6 ('all our righteousnesses are like filthy rags'). The apparent contradiction between these two statements is resolved when we realise that they are dealing with different concerns, the righteousness of the cause in the one case and that of the individual in the other. Psalm 7 speaks of the former; Isaiah 64 of the latter.

Matthew 10:9, 10 ('Provide neither gold . . . nor sandals, nor staffs') and Mark 6:8, 9 ('take nothing . . . except a staff . . . but . . . wear sandals') provide us with another example. Here the texts seem to contradict one another unless we recognise that Matthew's account speaks of a staff as a burden to its bearers, while Mark is thinking of a staff's value in sustaining and easing the journey of a traveller – such as Jacob used (*Gen.* 32:10). Again, the shoes that Matthew mentions are new ones, carefully packed for travel. By contrast the sandals in Mark are not new, but are the kind that would have been daily worn on the feet.

Various conditions and caveats should be observed here in harmonising biblical passages.

(i) The writers of Scripture sometimes speak of places and people from the past in terms of the customs of the time and place in which they themselves wrote. An example of this is found in Genesis 12:8: 'And he moved from there to the mountain east of Bethel'. The place was called Bethel in the days of Moses; but in Abraham's time it was called Luz (*Gen.* 28:19). Genesis 13:1 records that 'Abraham went up from Egypt . . . to the south'. Here 'south' does not mean 'south from Egypt', but south of where Moses was when he wrote. Again, we are told that Christ in his Spirit preached to those in prison (*1 Pet.* 3:19). They are said to be in prison with respect to the time when Peter wrote his letter, not the time in which Noah lived. Again, in the context of the patriarchs, God says in Psalm 105:15: 'Do not touch My anointed ones.' The experience of Abraham, Isaac and Jacob is here being described in terms of the ritual of the days in which David lived. The patriarchs did not receive external anointing.

(ii) Allegories or passages marked by literary symbolism should be expounded according to the scope or focus of the context. Thus Chrysostom says on Matthew 8: 'Parables must not be expounded according to the letter, lest many absurdities follow.' Similarly, Augustine says in connection with Psalm 8: 'In every allegory this rule is to be retained, that that be considered according to the purpose of the present place, which is there spoken of under a similitude.'

(iii) The same places and people in Scripture may have two different names. Gideon was called both Jerubbaal (*Judg.* 6:32) and Jerubbesheth (*2 Sam.* 11:21). Then the same name may appear in different forms. So, Salmon (*Ruth* 4:21) is called Salmah [Solomon] (*2 Chron.* 2:11). On the other hand, different people and places may share the same name. One example of this is found in the genealogy with which Matthew's Gospel begins: 'Josiah begot Jeconiah and his brothers about the time they were carried away to Babylon. And after they were brought to Babylon, Jeconiah begot Shealtiel' (*Matt.* 1:11, 12). The name 'Jeconiah' concludes the second of the three groups of fourteen into which the genealogy is divided and also begins the third. If this is the same individual, there must be only thirteen people in either the second or the third group. But if there were two men called Jeconiah, a father and son, the problem is resolved.

Succoth is the name of three different places in Scripture. The first is in Egypt (*Exod.* 12:37); the second is in the land of the tribe of Gad (*Josh.* 13:27); the third in the land of the tribe of Manasseh (*1 Kings* 7:46).

(iv) Sometimes in Scripture, because of the sinful life-style of a ruler his name or the number of years during which he reigned wickedly may be omitted. 'Saul reigned two years over Israel' (*1 Sam.* 13:1); that is, lawfully, or as Lyra says, *de jure* (according to law or equity); but otherwise he reigned longer. We have a further example in Matthew 1:8: 'Joram begot Uzziah.' Here three kings are simply omitted because of their wickedness, namely Ahaziah, Joash and Amaziah.

(v) Time periods may be noted in complete or in-complete form. They may also be reckoned inclusively or exclusively. There is an example of this in 1 Kings 15:25 and 1 Kings 15:28. Nadab, who began to reign in the *second year* of Asa can be said to reign two years, although Baasha is said to have succeeded him in the *third year* of Asa. Obviously the final 'year' of a king's reign did not last for a complete year, since it was cut short by his death. On occasion (as here) the last 'year' might scarcely last a month or more. The remainder of the year would then count as a complete 'year' of the reign of any successor.

We find another apparent contradiction in chronology if we compare Matthew 17:1 with Luke 9:28. But this is resolved if we recognise that Matthew is counting only complete days while Luke also includes the part days on either side of them. Thus, despite appearances, there is no real contradiction between Matthew's 'six days' and Luke's 'about eight days'. Sometimes a time period is numbered inclusively and sometimes exclusively. There may be various reasons for this, it may simply be a prefer-ence for using a perfect number. Augustine says on Exodus, 'In a perfect number oft-times that, which is either wanting or abounding, is not counted.' Thus, for example: 'While Israel dwelt in Heshbon and its villages, in Aroer and its villages . . . for three hundred years' (*Judg.* 11:26). These years from the departure of the Israelites out of Egypt, can be calculated as follows:

The wilderness wandering:	40 years
The leadership of Joshua:	17 years
Of Othniel:	40 years
Of Ehud and Shamgar:	80 years
Of Barak:	40 years
Of Gideon:	40 years
Of Abimelech:	3 years
Of Tola:	23 years
Of Jair:	22 years

The total is 305 years (not 300). The reason the extra five years are not mentioned is simply because the round number is easier to work with.

Again, a round number may be used simply for brevity: 'So all who fell of Benjamin that day were twenty-five thousand men' (*Judg.* 20:46). Here (as a glance at Judges 20:35 will indicate) a hundred Benjamites are not included.

(vi) A further consideration in interpreting the narratives of Old Testament history is the fact that when a king was hindered from exercising his role within the nation either by foreign war or old age, or because of some disease, he might appoint his son king in his place while he was still alive. In such co-regencies the calculations of the length of the reigns of the father and son sometimes include the years of joint reign, but at other times take account only of the years of the individual's reign.

This helps to resolve the difference between 2 Kings 1:17 and 2 Kings 3:1. In the seventeenth year of his reign Jehoshaphat determined to help king Ahab against the

Syrians, and appointed his son Joram to be viceroy. In the eighteenth year of Jehoshaphat's reign (the second of his son's) Joram the son of Ahab reigned. Afterwards in the fifth year of Joram the son of Ahab, Jehoshaphat, now languishing in old age, confirmed his kingdom to Joram, who is then said to have reigned eight years: four while his father was alive, and four by himself after the death of his father.

Another illustration will be found by comparing 2 Kings 15:30 (which implies that Jotham reigned for twenty years) with 2 Kings 15:33 (which suggests that he reigned for only sixteen years). The difficulty is easily resolved. Jotham reigned for sixteen years on his own after the death of his father Uzziah; but in addition he reigned for four further years along with his father (i.e. twenty years in total) since he governed the kingdom for his father when the latter had leprosy.

(vii) In the ancient Near-East, the day was artificially divided both into 12 equal hours (commonly called planetary hours, cf. *John* 11:9) and into quadrants, each of which was denoted by the number of the hour with which the period began. This enables us to harmonise Mark 15:25 which says that Jesus was crucified at 'the third hour' with John 19:14 which states that it was already 'about the sixth hour' when Pilate presented Jesus to the Jews. These two numbers belong to different frames of reference. Different ways of counting the hours of the day are in view. Hence Christ may be said to have been crucified at the *third* hour, although he had not yet been taken to Golgotha at the *sixth* hour.

(viii) A lesser number is included in a greater and more complete number. 'So the land had rest for forty years. Then Othniel the son of Kenaz died' (*Judg.* 3:11). This figure includes the years reckoned from the death of Joshua to the death of Othniel, as well as the eight years of bondage under the Syrians. 'The land had rest for eighty years' (*Judg.* 3:30). Here from the death of Othniel are included the years of both Ehud and Shamgar. For Ehud could not have been judge for eighty years which would be more than a lifespan. Similar instances occur in Judges 5:31; 8:28; 9:22; 10:2,3 and 11:26 where the forty years of the wanderings in the desert are included in the figure of three hundred years.

(ix) Sonship can be either natural or legal. Natural sonship is by generation, while legal is by adoption, testified by education and upbringing, and by succession in the kingdom, and also, in the case of levirate sonship by the law of redemption (see *Deut.* 25:5).

5. When the natural sense of a passage can be determined with the help of these principles, the meaning which is most appropriate to the context should be assumed for any word which is open to a range of meaning.

Thus, for example, the Hebrew word for 'and', *waw*, can be translated in a variety of ways, according to the context – as: 'but', 'since', 'indeed', 'that is', 'for that reason', 'so', and by many similar terms.[1]

Again, the Hebrew word *barak* can indicate such opposite ideas as to bless and to curse (*Job* 1:5; *1 Kings* 21:10 and 11:2, 9). And *chalal* in Genesis 4:26 does not mean 'profane' (as it sometimes does) but 'begin', for two reasons. (i) When it means to profane it should be joined with the noun which it governs; but here it is followed immediately by the infinitive of the verb to call, *qara*. (ii) Moses did not count the profanation of the worship of God as one of the reasons for the flood; but that would

---

[1] Perkins lists a total of thirty-seven different examples of the nuances of meaning which the Hebrew word may have. The list is not printed here.

certainly have been noted if it had been prevalent among the people of God.

6.   In our English Bibles, marginal references some-times mention a Greek or Hebrew word indicating that there is some variation in the extant manuscripts of the passage. The correct reading is the one which (i) agrees with the grammatical construction, and with other reliable manuscripts. (ii) makes sense of the context and thrust of the passage and agrees with the analogy of faith.

I mention this as a principle of interpretation, not because I think that our copies of the Hebrew and Greek text were corrupted through the malicious activity of the Jews, as Lindanus (followed by the Roman Church) argues. I mention it simply so that the various readings – which have arisen either through a lack of skill or negligence and oversight on the part of those who made copies of the text – might be scanned and the correct reading determined.

For example, in most copies of the Hebrew text, Psalm 22:16 reads *kaari*, meaning '*As a lion* my hands and my feet.' But in some copies of the Hebrew the reading is different: *kaaru*, '*They have digged (or pierced)* my hands and my feet.' The rule we have adopted would indicate that the latter reading is to be followed since it agrees with (i) the grammatical construction; (ii) the circum-stances of the psalm; (iii) some ancient copies, as the Jews themselves recognise.

6. *Rightly Handling the Word of God*

So far we have been considering the interpretation of Scripture. Now we come to consider the right 'cutting', or 'dividing' of it. Right cutting is the way in which the Word is enabled to edify the people of God: 'Be diligent to present yourself approved to God, a worker who does not need to be ashamed, rightly dividing [or cutting] the word of truth' (*2 Tim.* 2:15).

The idea of cutting here is metaphorical language possibly derived from the activity of the Levites, who were required to cut the limbs of the animals they sacrificed with great care. It is of this skill that the Messiah speaks: 'The Lord God has given Me the tongue of the learned, That I should know how to speak a word in season to him who is weary' (*Isa.* 50:4).

There are two elements in this: (i) resolution or partition, and (ii) application.

Resolution

Resolution is the unfolding of the passage into its various doctrines, like the untwisting and loosening of a weaver's web. Apollos was highly skilled in doing this: 'for he vigorously refuted the Jews publicly, showing from the Scriptures that Jesus is the Christ' (*Acts* 18:28).

Sometimes the doctrine is explicitly stated in the passage. This is already illustrated in New Testament references to the Old Testament: 'We have previously charged both Jews and Greeks that they are all under sin. As it is written: There is none righteous, no, not one; There is none who understands; There is none who seeks after God. They have all turned aside; They have together become unprofitable; There is none who does good, no, not one' (*Rom.* 3:9–11). Another example is found in Acts 2:24–27.

On other occasions a doctrine not specifically stated is correctly drawn from the text because, in one sense or another, it is implied in what is written. There are many illustrations of how this is done in Scripture itself. For example:

BIBLICAL TEXT	IMPLICATION DRAWN FROM THE TEXT
Example 1 John 10:34: Jesus answered them, 'Is it not written in your law, "I said, you are gods"'?	John 10:35: If He called them gods to whom the word of God came (and the Scripture cannot be broken): 36: Do you say of Him whom the Father sanctified and sent into the world, 'You are blaspheming', because I said, 'I am the Son of God'?
Example 2 1 Corinthians 9:9: For it is written in the law of Moses, 'You shall not muzzle an ox while it treads out the grain.' Is it oxen God is concerned about?	1 Corinthians 9:4: Do we have no right to eat and drink?

Example 3

Galatians 3:10: For as many as are of the works of the law are under the curse; for it is written, 'Cursed is everyone who does not continue in all things which are written in the book of the law, to do them.'

Galatians 3:9: So then those who are of faith are blessed with believing Abraham.

Example 4

Galatians 3:11: For 'the just shall live by faith'.

Galatians 3:11: But that no one is justified by the law in the sight of God is evident.

Example 5

Hebrews 8:8: Because finding fault with them, He says: 'Behold, the days are coming, says the Lord, when I will make a new covenant with the house of Israel and with the house of Judah'.

Hebrews 8:13: In that He says, 'A new covenant', He has made the first obsolete. Now what is becoming obsolete and growing old is ready to vanish away.

In elucidating doctrines we must bear in mind that an example that is ethical, economic, political, ordinary or extraordinary has the force of a general rule within its own sphere. The examples of the fathers are patterns for us, as Paul indicates: 'Now all these things . . . were written for our admonition' (*1 Cor.* 10:11). It is a principle in logic that the genus is present in all the species, just as it is a rule in visual perception that the general species of things are perceived before the particular.

Example 6

Romans 9:7: Nor are they all children because they are the seed of Abraham; but, 'In Isaac your seed shall be called'. 10: And not only this, but when Rebecca also had conceived by one man, even by our father Isaac . . .

Romans 9:8: That is, those who are the children of the flesh, these are not the children of God; but the children of the promise are counted as the seed.

Example 7

Romans 4:18: Abraham, contrary to hope, etc. 21: Being fully convinced that what He had promised He was also able to perform. 22: And therefore 'it was accounted to him for righteousness.'

Romans 4:23: Now it was not written for his sake alone that it was imputed to him. 24: But also for us. It shall be imputed to us who believe in Him who raised up Jesus our Lord from the dead.

Note, however, that doctrines ought to be deduced from passages only when it is proper and valid to do so. They must be derived from the genuine meaning of the Scripture. Otherwise we will end up drawing any doctrine from any place in the Bible.

An example of such a mistake is the way in which Proverbs 8:22 has been handled. In this passage Wisdom, that is Christ, is speaking about himself. According to the Septuagint (the Greek translation of the Old Testament) the passage reads: 'The Lord has created me.' From this translation the Arians[1] perversely argued that the Son

---

[1] Followers of Arius (c.250–c.336).

was created. But the Hebrew text reads: 'The Lord has *possessed* me' (the Hebrew verb is *qanah*). The Father *possesses* the Son, because he was begotten of the Father from eternity, and because the Father is in the Son, and the Son in the Father. And so when a son was born to Adam he said he had '*possessed* a man from the Lord' (*Gen.* 4:1; again the Hebrew verb is *qanah*). The error here perhaps arose because of a scribal error (accidental or deliberate) in the Greek text.

In the same way, Augustine comments on Psalm 39:10, reading the text: 'I held my peace because thou hast made me.' He makes the subtle application that it is a marvel that he – who had been given a mouth to enable him to speak – should hold his tongue. But the word 'me' is in neither the Hebrew nor the Greek text. Again, in his comments on Psalm 72:14 he discusses the question of money-lending for interest and proves that this is sinful. But there is nothing about this in the text! It reads: 'He will redeem their life from oppression and violence; And precious shall be their blood in His sight.'

It is also legitimate to develop analogies or allegories. These are arguments drawn from things that are like each other. Paul used them often (e.g. *1 Cor.* 9:9). But they are to be employed with the following caveats:

1. They should be used sparingly and soberly.

2. They must not be far-fetched, but appropriate to the matter in hand.

3. They must be mentioned briefly.

4. They should be used for practical instruction not to prove a point of doctrine.

Any point of doctrine drawn from a text by proper interpretation should be believed on its own authority. This is an adequate basis for believing it. 'Now a certain Jew named Apollos, born at Alexandria, an eloquent man and mighty in the Scriptures, came to Ephesus . . . for he vigorously refuted the Jews publicly, showing from the Scriptures that Jesus is the Christ' (*Acts* 18:24, 28). It follows from this that:

1. We should not rest our faith on human testimonies, either from the philosophers, or the Fathers. Augustine comments on Psalm 66 thus: 'If I speak, let no man hear; if Christ speak, woe be to him that does not hear.' Again he says, 'Let us not hear, "these things I say, these things he says": but let us hear, "These things the Lord says".' Yet with this exception: 'Unless they convince the conscience of the hearer.' It was in this way that Paul appealed to the testimony of Aratus, 'For in Him we live and move and have our being, as also some of your own poets have said; "For we are also His offspring. Therefore, since we are the offspring of God . . ."' (*Acts* 17:28, 29). Similarly he cites the saying of Menander, 'Do not be deceived: "Evil company corrupts good habits"' (*1 Cor.* 15:33). Again, he quotes Epimenides: 'One of them, a prophet of their own, said, "Cretans are always liars, evil beasts, lazy gluttons"' (*Titus* 1:12).

But if such secular authors are quoted, it must be sparingly. In fact the biblical precedents actually omit the names of the authors in such instances.

2. Only a few testimonies of Scripture should be used for the proof of the doctrine; sometimes there is need of none.

3. The prophets who expound their teaching in this way are not to be criticised by other prophets (see *1 Cor.* 14:32, 37).

7. Use and Application

Application is the skill by which the doctrine which has been properly drawn from Scripture is handled in ways which are appropriate to the circumstances of the place and time and to the people in the congregation. This is the biblical approach to exposition: '"I will feed My flock, and I will make them lie down," says the Lord God. "I will seek what was lost and bring back what was driven away, bind up the broken and strengthen what was sick"' (*Ezek.* 34:15, 16). 'And on some have compassion, making a distinction, but others save with fear, pulling them out of the fire' (*Jude* 22, 23).

The basic principle in application is to know whether the passage is a statement of the law or of the gospel. For when the Word is preached, the law and the gospel operate differently. The law exposes the disease of sin, and as a side-effect stimulates and stirs it up. But it provides no remedy for it. However the gospel not only teaches us what is to be done, it also has the power of the Holy Spirit joined to it. When we are regenerated by him we receive the strength we need both to believe the gospel and to do what it commands. The law is, therefore, first in the order of teaching; then comes the gospel.

A statement of the law indicates the need for perfect inherent righteousness, of eternal life given through the works of the law, of the sins which are contrary to the law and of the curse that is due them. 'For as many as are of the works of the law are under the curse; for it is written, "Cursed is everyone who does not continue in all things which are written in the book of the law, to do them." But that no one is justified by the law in the sight of God is evident, for the just shall live by faith' (*Gal.* 3:10). 'Brood of vipers! Who warned you to flee from the wrath to come . . . And even now the axe is laid to the root of the trees. Therefore every tree which does not bear good fruit is cut down and thrown into the fire' (*Matt.* 3:7, 10). By contrast, a statement of the gospel speaks of Christ and his benefits, and of faith being fruitful in good works. For example, 'For God so loved the world that He gave His only begotten Son, that whoever believes in Him should not perish but have everlasting life' (*John* 3:16).

For this reason many statements which seem to belong to the law are, in the light of Christ, to be understood not legally but as qualified by the gospel. 'Blessed are those who hear the word of God and keep it!' (*Luke* 11:28). 'For this commandment which I command you today is not too mysterious for you, nor is it far off . . . But the word is very near you, in your mouth and in your heart, that you may do it' (*Deut.* 30:11, 14). This same sentence which is legal in character in Moses, is evangelical in character in Paul (*Rom.* 10:8). 'Blessed are the undefiled in the way, Who walk in the law of the Lord! Blessed are those who keep His testimonies, Who seek Him with the whole heart!' (*Psa.* 119:1, 2). 'He who has My commandments and keeps them, it is he who loves Me, And he who loves Me will be loved by My Father . . . If anyone loves Me, he will keep My word; and My Father will love him, and We will come to him and make Our home with him' (*John* 14:21, 23). 'Noah was a just man, perfect in his generations, Noah walked with God' (*Gen.* 6:9). 'I am Almighty God; walk before Me and be blameless' (*Gen.* 17:1).

There are basically seven ways in which application should be made, in keeping with seven different spiritual conditions.

Categories of Hearers

1. Those who are unbelievers and are both ignorant and unteachable. These must first of all be prepared to receive the doctrine of the Word. Jehoshaphat sent Levites throughout the cities of Judah to teach the people, and to draw them away from idolatry (*2 Chron.* 17:9). This preparation should be partly by discussing or reasoning with them, in order to become aware of their attitude and disposition, and partly by reproving any obvious sin, so that their consciences may be aroused and touched with fear and they may become teachable (see *Acts* 9:3-5; 16:27–31; 17:17; 17:22–24).

When there is some hope that they have become teachable and prepared, the message of God's Word is to be given to them, usually in basic terms concentrating on general points (as, for example, Paul did at Athens, *Acts* 17:30, 31). If there is no positive response to such teaching, then it should be explained in a more detailed and comprehensive way. But if they remain unteachable and there is no real hope of winning them, they should simply be left (*Prov.* 9:8; *Matt.* 7:6; *Acts* 19:9).

2. Those who are teachable, but ignorant. We should instruct such people by means of a catechism (cf. *Luke* 1:4; *Acts* 18:25, 26). A catechism is a brief explanation of the foundational teaching of the Christian faith given in the form of questions and answers. This helps both the understanding and the memory. The content of a catechism, therefore, should be the fundamentals of the Christian faith, a summary of its basic principles (*Heb.* 5:12).

A principle of the faith is a biblical truth which is

directly and immediately concerned both with the salvation of men and the glory of God. If it is denied and rejected there are no grounds for us to hope for salvation. There are six such principles: repentance, faith, baptism (that is the sacraments), the laying on of hands (that is a synecdoche for the ministry of the Word), the resurrection, and the last judgment (*Heb.* 6:1-3).

The distinctive form of a catechism is the way it handles the elements or foundation points plainly by question and answer (*Acts* 8:37; *1 Pet.* 3:21). As Tertullian put it, 'The soul is not purged with washing, but with answering.'

Here it is important to recognise the difference between 'milk' and 'strong meat'. These categories refer to the same truth; the difference between them lies in the manner and style of the teaching. 'Milk' is a brief, plain and general explanation of the principles of the faith: that we must believe in one God, and in three persons, Father, Son and Holy Spirit; that we must rely only upon the grace of God in Christ; that we ought to believe in the forgiveness of sins; and when we are taught that we ought to repent, to abstain from evil and to do good.

'Strong meat', on the other hand, is a detailed, full, illuminating and clear handling of the doctrine of faith. It includes careful and lucid exposition of biblical teaching on such themes as: the condition of man before the fall, the fall, original and actual sin, human guilt, free-will; the mysteries of the Trinity, the two natures of Christ, their union in one person, the office of Christ as Mediator, the imputation of righteousness; faith, grace, and the use of the law. 'Milk' must be set before babes, that is those who are immature or weak in knowledge; strong meat should be given to those who are more mature, that is to those who are better instructed (*1 Cor.* 3:1, 2; *Heb.* 5:13).

3. There are those who have knowledge, but have never been humbled. Here we need to see the foundation of repentance stirred up in what Paul calls godly sorrow (*1 Cor.* 7:8–10). Godly sorrow is grief for sin simply because it is sin. To stir up this affection, the ministry of the law is necessary. This may give birth to a real sense of contrition in the heart, or to terror in the conscience. Although this is not wholesome and profitable on its own, it provides a necessary remedy for subduing sinful stubbornness, and for preparing the mind to become teachable.

In order to arouse this legal sorrow it is appropriate to use some choice section of the law, which may reprove any obvious sin in those who have not yet been humbled. Sorrow for and repentance from even one sin is in substance sorrow for and repentance of all sin (*Psa.* 32:5; *Acts* 2:23, 8:22).

Further, if someone who is afflicted with the cross and with outward tragedies has only a worldly sorrow – that is if he does not mourn for sin *as sin*, but only for the punishment of sin – he is not to be given immediate comfort. Such sorrow must first be transformed into godly sorrow. Think about the analogy of medical healing. If a man's life is in danger because of the amount of blood he is losing from a nose-bleed, his physicians may prescribe that blood be let out of his arm, or from some other suitable place, in order to staunch the flow of blood from his nose. Their motive, of course, is to save someone who is in danger of death.

Then let the gospel be preached in such a way that the Holy Spirit effectually works salvation. For in renewing men so that they may begin to will and to do what is pleasing to God, the Spirit really and truly produces in them godly sorrow and repentance to salvation.

To the hard-hearted the law must be stressed, and its

curse stated clearly along with its threats. The difficulty of obtaining deliverance until people are pricked in their heart should also be taught (*Matt.* 3:7; 19:16, 17; 23:13, 33). But when the beginning of genuine sorrow appears they are to be comforted with the gospel.

4. Those who have already been humbled. Here we must carefully consider whether the humbling that has already taken place is complete and sound or only just begun and still light or superficial. It is important that people do not receive comfort sooner than is appropriate. If they do they may later become hardened in the same way iron which has been cast into the furnace becomes exceptionally hard when it is cold.

Here are some guidelines for dealing with those who are partially humbled. Expound the law to them carefully tempered with the gospel, so that being terrified by their sins and the judgment of God they may at the same time find comfort in the gospel (*Gen.* 3:9–15; *2 Sam.* 12; *Acts* 8:20–23). Nathan gives us an example here. Having been sent from God, he recalled David to an awareness of his true condition through a parable, and then pronounced him pardoned when his repentance was certain.

In this way faith and repentance and the comforts of the gospel ought to be taught and offered to those who have been fully humbled (*Matt.* 9:13; *Luke* 4:18; *Acts* 2:37, 38).

5. Those who already believe. We must teach them:

(i) The gospel: the biblical teaching on justification, sanctification and perseverance.

(ii) The law: but as it applies to those who are no longer under its curse, so that they may be taught how to bear the fruit of a new obedience in keeping with their repentance (*Rom.* 8:1; *1 Tim.* 1:9). Here Paul's teaching in Romans serves as a model.

(iii) Although someone who is righteous and holy in the sight of God should not be threatened with the curse of the law, the opposition of the law to their remaining sin should still be stressed. As a father may show his sons what he will do as punishment to induce a proper sense of fear of doing wrong, so meditation on the curse of the law should be frequently encouraged in true believers, to discourage abusing the mercy of God by sinful living, and to increase humility. Our sanctification is partial as yet. In order that the remnants of sin may be destroyed we must always begin with meditation on the law, and with a sense of our sin, in order to be brought to rest in the gospel.

6.   Those who have fallen back. Some may have partly departed from the state of grace, either in faith or in life-style.

Failure in faith is either in the knowledge of the doctrine of the gospel or in apprehending Christ.

Failure in knowledge involves declining into error, whether in a secondary or fundamental doctrine.

In this situation, the specific doctrine which counteracts their error should be expounded and taught. We need to stress its importance to them, along with the doctrine of repentance. But we must do this with a brotherly affection, as Paul says in Galatians 6:1 (cf. *2 Tim.* 2:25).

A fall from apprehending Christ leads to despair. In order to restore such we need to diagnose their condition and then prescribe the remedy. We must analyse either the cause of their temptation or of their condition. The diagnosis of the cause can be done appropriately by private confession (cf. *James* 5:17). But to prevent such confession being turned into an instrument of torture it must be governed by these principles:

(i)   It ought to be done freely and not under any compulsion. Salvation does not depend on it.

(ii)   It must not be a confession of all sins, but only of those which eat at the conscience and may lead to even greater spiritual danger if they are not dealt with.

(iii)   Such confession should chiefly be made to pastors, but with the understanding that it may be confidentially shared with other reliable men in the church.

The diagnosis of a person's spiritual status involves investigating whether they are under the law or under grace. In order to clarify this we must probe and question to discover from them whether they are displeased with themselves, because they have displeased God. Do they hate sin *as sin*? That is the foundation of the repentance which brings salvation. Then, secondly we must ask whether they have or feel in their heart a desire to be reconciled with God. This is the groundwork for a living faith.

When the diagnosis is complete, the remedy must be prescribed and applied from the gospel. It is twofold.

Firstly, several gospel truths must be explained and frequently impressed upon them, including:

(i)   That their sin is pardonable.

(ii)   That the promises of grace are made generally to all who believe. They are not made to specific individuals; they therefore exclude no-one.

(iii)   That the will to believe is itself faith (*Psa.* 145:19; *Rev.* 21:6).

(iv)   That sin does not abolish grace but rather (since God turns everything to the good of those who are his) can lead to further illustrations of it.

(v)   That in this fallen and sinful world all of God's works are done by means which are contrary to him!

Secondly, they must be encouraged, in the very bitterness of the temptation, to stir up the faith which has been lying idle – but covered over as it were. They must reassure themselves that their sins are forgiven. And they must be encouraged to struggle vigorously in prayer, either alone or with others, against carnal sense and human hope. They must be exhorted with great earnestness in order to enable them to do these things; even those who are unwilling must somehow be constrained to do them (see *Psalms* 77:1, 2; 130:1, 2; *Rom.* 4:18).

So that such remedies may do their work, the ministerial power of 'binding and loosing' is to be used in the form prescribed in the Scriptures (*2 Sam.* 12:13; *2 Cor.* 5:20). If by any chance melancholy troubles the individual's mind then a remedy for it must be sought in private.

Failure in life-style takes place when a Christian commits actual sin, as in the case of Noah's drunkenness, David's adultery, Peter's denial and similar examples. The strength and disposition of indwelling grace may be lost for a time in terms of both the sense and the experience of the power of it. The law must be expounded along with the gospel to those who have thus fallen. Every new act of sin requires a new act of faith and repentance (*Isa.* 1:4, 16, 18).

7. Churches with both believers and unbelievers. This is the typical situation in our congregations. Any doctrine may be expounded to them, either from the law or from the gospel, so long as its biblical limitations and circumscriptions are observed (see *John* 7:37). This was what the prophets did in their sermons, when they announced judgment and destruction on the wicked, and promised deliverance in the Messiah to those who repented.

But what if someone in the congregation despairs,

when the rest are hardened? What should be done? The answer is: those who are hardened must be made to hear the law circumscribed within the limits of the persons and the sins in view. But the afflicted conscience must be helped to hear the voice of the gospel applied especially to it.

8. *Varieties of Application*

Application is of two kinds, mental and practical.

Mental Application
Mental application is concerned with the mind and involves either doctrine or reproof (*2 Tim.* 3:16, 17).

When it involves doctrine, biblical teaching is used to inform the mind to enable it to come to a right judgment about what is to be believed. Reproof is using biblical teaching in order to recover the mind from error.

When false teaching is refuted during the exposition of Scripture the following cautions should be observed.

1. Make sure that you thoroughly understand the issue involved, or 'the state of the question' to be discussed.

2. Reprove only the errors which currently trouble the church. Leave others alone if they lie dead in past history, or if they are not relevant to the people, unless you know that spiritual danger may still arise from them. This was the situation described in Revelation chapter two when the church at Pergamos was warned to beware of the Nicolaitans whose teaching had already influenced some of them.

3. If the error is not foundational to the gospel, the refutation should be done not only in a truly Christian

fashion (as should always be the case) but also in a friendly manner. Gentle and brotherly disagreement is called for here.

Practical Application

Practical application has to do with life-style and behaviour and involves instruction and correction.

Instruction is the application of doctrine to enable us to live well in the context of the family, the state and the church. It involves both encouragement and exhortation (*Rom.* 15:4).

Correction is the application of doctrine in a way that transforms lives marked by ungodliness and unrighteousness. This involves admonition. Such admonition must be done generally at first, without reference to specific circumstances. This principle is well-illustrated in 2 Samuel 12 where Nathan first made David aware of his sin by means of a general parable. Paul appears to have adopted a similar approach (see *Acts* 19:26, 35, 37).

If this kind of reproof does not bear fruit, it should be expressed in more detailed ways (see *1 Tim.* 5:20). But our expressions of hatred for sin must always be accompanied by an obvious love for the person who has sinned. Whenever possible the minister should include himself in his reproofs. In this way his preaching, teaching and counselling will be expressed in a mild and gentle spirit (cf. *Dan.* 4:16-19; *1 Cor.* 4:6; *Gal.* 2:15).

These different kinds of application can be employed with respect to every sentence of the Scripture. But it may be valuable to use an example drawing on what Matthias Flacius Illyricus (1520–75), the Lutheran, has written on Matthew 10:28 where Jesus urges the disciples not to fear those who can kill only the body, but rather to fear him who can destroy both body and soul in hell.

It would be easy to elicit a wide variety of doctrines

from this text, in relation to both our confession of faith and God's providence.

Doctrine

1. It is necessary for us to confess publicly the doctrine we know whenever the need arises.

2. We must make this confession even if it means risking the loss of our possessions and our lives.

3. We should despise the value of our lives by comparison with the value we place on Christ and his truth.

4. Eternal punishments which will be experienced both in soul and body are prepared for those who are not afraid to deny Christ and his truth.

5. God is intent and ready to rule and guide us, to enable us to make our confession aright.

6. The providence of God is not only general, but also particular, and includes the tiniest details, even the hairs of our head!

Reproof

1. It is a mistake to think it is adequate merely to embrace in the heart the faith and right views of religion. It is equally mistaken to imagine that it is within human power in the meantime to grant or affirm anything before men, such as the condition of the place, time and persons requires, especially when life seems to be in imminent danger of ending.

2. Epicureans are in error when they deny divine providence, thinking it beneath the majesty of God to take care of human affairs.

3. Stoics are in error when they imagine that all things are governed by fate (or by some irresistible and violent necessity).

4. Those who displace the wise ordination of the divine providence with chance and fortune are also mistaken.

5. Pelagians are in error in attributing more than is warranted to man's strength, as though it were in men's power to embrace the faith at their own pleasure or to continue steadfastly in it and fearlessly confess it to the end.

6. Others err when they depend more on outward things and unstable riches than on the power and goodness of God.

Instruction

1. You must, to the full extent of your power, strive to have a true fear of God in view, because you have now learned that the one God is to be feared above all men.

2. You must learn to despise human things to such an extent that you always desire, having forsaken them, to leave this world and be with Christ in heaven.

3. The consideration of God's special providence should teach you to think of the presence of God as all-seeing and all-knowing, to seek his help, and also to believe that you are helped in all things, and finally that there is no danger so terrible but he is able and willing to deliver you from it, when it is fit.

Correction

1. These words of Christ correct the negligence of those who do not pray for sincere love, so that inflamed with it they would not refuse to lay down their life for his name.

2. There is here, too, a criticism of the negligence of those who do not acknowledge or see the providence of God showing itself in all things.

3.   There is reproof here for those who do not give God thanks for promising in his providence to govern and defend us in everything that concerns us.

4.   Those who abuse God's good creation are rebuked here since it is clear that God takes care of all things.

Any passage in Scripture can be handled in this way. Note, however, that we should not try to expound every doctrine on every occasion; but only those which can be applied appropriately to the present experiences and condition of the church. These must be carefully chosen, and limited to a few, lest those who hear God's Word expounded are overwhelmed by the sheer number of applications.

9. *The Use of the Memory*

Because it is customary to preach directly from the heart (or memory), something should be said here in connection with the use of the memory.

Artificial memory aids,[1] like those which depend on remembering places and images can teach us how to commit sermons to memory easily, but they cannot be approved, for several reasons:

1. Memory aids which involve the stimulation of an image to trigger the memory involve us in an unspiritual activity. Such a method requires absurd, unworthy and, actually, monstrous thoughts. That is especially true of those which heighten and inflame the most corrupt affections of the flesh.

2. Artificial ways of remembering dull the mind and the memory. They require a threefold rather than a single

---

[1] The use of such artificial aids in public speech had been discussed in classical and medieval times. Perkins has in mind here the 'memory systems' taught by the Italian, Giordano Bruno and the Scot, Alexander Dickson, against whom he had written two tracts in 1584. These artificial aids relied on the use of images and the occult while others urged the development of the passions by the use of memory. There is some evidence that before his conversion Perkins himself had a fascination with the occult.

memory: first remembering the places, then the images, and then thirdly what is actually to be said.

It is more helpful if when preparing for preaching we carefully imprint on our mind – with the help of an axiomatical, syllogistical, or methodical way of thinking – the various proofs and applications of the doctrines, the illustrations of the applications, and the order in which we plan to expound them. There is no need to be overly anxious about the precise words we will use. As Horace says, words 'will not unwillingly follow the matter that is premeditated'.

The practice of memorising a sermon manuscript word for word has many disadvantages. For one thing, it involves an enormous amount of work. For another, if in our anxiety we lose the place then the congregation is in difficulties and our own mind ends up in a state of confusion. In addition, this practice hinders freedom of pronunciation, action and the Spirit-given flow of spiritual affections, because our minds are almost obsessed with whether our memory – which we have burdened with so much information – is going to fail us.

10. *Preaching the Word*

We have discussed the preparation of the substance of the sermon. Now we must think about the actual preaching itself. Here two things are essential: (i) the hiding of human wisdom, and (ii) the demonstration or manifestation of the Spirit. Human wisdom must be concealed, both in the content of the sermon and in the language we use. The preaching of the Word is the testimony of God and the profession of the knowledge of Christ, not of human skill. Furthermore, the hearers ought not to ascribe their faith to the gifts of men, but to the power of God's Word (*1 Cor.* 2:1, 2, 5). But this does not mean that pulpits will be marked by a lack of knowledge and education. The minister may, and in fact *must*, privately make free use of the general arts and of philosophy as well as employ a wide variety of reading while he is preparing his sermon. But in public exposition these should be hidden from the congregation, not ostentatiously paraded before them. As the Latin proverb says, *Artis etiam celare artem* – it is also a point of art to conceal art.

The 'demonstration of the Spirit' (*1 Cor.* 2:4) becomes a reality when, in preaching, the minister of the Word conducts himself in such a way that everyone – even those who are ignorant of the gospel and are unbelievers – recognise that it is not so much the preacher who is speaking, but the Spirit of God in him and by him (*Mic.* 3:8; *1 Cor.* 2:4; 14:24, 25; 4:19, 20). This is what makes his ministry living and powerful (*Luke* 11:27).

Such a 'demonstration' will come to expression either in speech or in gesture. The speech must be spiritual and gracious. Spiritual speech is speech which the Holy Spirit teaches (*1 Cor.* 2:13). It is both simple and clear, tailored to the understanding of the hearers and appropriate for expressing the majesty of the Spirit (*Acts* 17:2, 3; *2 Cor.* 4:2–4; *Gal.* 3:1). For this reason none of the specialised vocabulary of the arts, nor Greek and Latin phrases, nor odd turns of phrase should be used in the sermon. These distract the minds of those listeners who cannot see the connection between what has been said and what follows. In addition, unusual words hinder rather than help people in their efforts to understand what is being said. And they also tend to draw their minds away from the subject in hand to other things. In this connection, too, mere story-telling as well as vulgar or foolish statements must be avoided.

Gracious speech expresses the grace of the heart (*Luke* 4:22; *John* 7:46). Such grace is either of the person, or of the ministry.

The grace of the person is the holiness of the heart and of an unblameable life. While these do not in themselves qualify anyone to be a minister, no-one can do the work of the ministry without them, for several reasons.

1.   Because the doctrine of the Word is hard to understand and to practise. Consequently the minister ought to express what he teaches by his example, as a kind of model or type of his own message (*Phil.* 4:8; *1 Tim.* 4:12; *1 Pet.* 5:3).

2.   A person is not godly, however much he may understand the Scriptures, if he does not possess an inward

sense and experience of the Word in his heart (*Gen.* 18:17–19; *Psa.* 25:8, 9; *Amos* 3:7).

3. God abhors godly speech which is not joined with a godly life (*Psa.* 50:16, 17). As Gregory of Nazianzus (c.329–c.389) said, it is as strange to see someone who is supposed to guide others on the way wandering out of the way himself, as it is to see a physician with signs of disease in his own body.

4. It is one of the secrets of ministry that the minister ought to cover his infirmities, so that they are not obvious. Ordinary people do not distinguish between the ministry and the minister. They are not able to see the importance of the ministry without first assessing the person of the minister. Herod heard John Baptist willingly, not because he was a good minister, but because he was a good man (*Mark* 6:20). Gregory of Nazianzus strikes the right note again when he says: 'He that teaches sound doctrine, and lives wickedly, reaches with one hand what he knocks away with the other.' John Chrysostom (347–407), commenting on Matthew 20, says: 'The doctor of the church by teaching well and by living well instructs the people how they ought to live well; but by living ill he instructs God how to condemn him.' And again: 'It is an easy matter to show wisdom in words; teach me to live by your life, this is the best teaching.' Words do not make as great an impression on the soul as works do!

5. A minister who is wicked, either openly or secretly, is not worthy to stand before the face of the most holy and almighty God (*Lev.* 10:3; *Isa.* 6:6–8; *Jer.* 15:19). That is why the judgments of God remain for wicked ministers to tremble at (*1 Sam.* 2:17, 25).

Holiness

Holiness involves the following elements as far as the preacher is concerned:

1. A good conscience (*Acts* 24:16; *2 Cor.* 1:12; *1 Tim.* 1:19). Without this, the mouth of the preacher will be closed (*Isa.* 56:10).

2. An inward sense of the doctrine we are to preach. Wood that is capable of burning is not set alight unless fire is put to it. Similarly anyone who would encourage godly affections and desires in others must first have godly affections himself. Thus, whatever responses a particular sermon requires should first be stirred up privately in our own minds, so that we can kindle the same flame in our hearers.

3. The fear of God, so that, filled with a reverent sense of the majesty of God, we will speak soberly and with moderation.

4. A love for the people (*1 Thess.* 2:7). To encourage this affection, the minister must pray seriously and fervently for the people of God (*1 Sam.* 12:23).

5. The minister must also be worthy of respect for his constancy, integrity, seriousness and truthfulness. He must know how to respect others in private or in public, in keeping with the character of his congregation.

6. He must be temperate, inwardly restraining any strong feelings. Both his outward style of behaviour and his gestures ought to be moderate and straightforward. In this way he will be marked by dignity and authority. Consequently he must be neither covetous, nor a heavy drinker, nor litigious, nor a pugnacious character, nor given to bursts of anger. Those who are younger men must devote themselves to godliness, and reject the lusts of youth (*1 Tim.* 4:7).

Grace

The grace of the minister consists of the following qualities:

1.   He must be able to teach (*1 Tim.* 3:2). Paul does not simply mean that it is highly desirable for this gift to be present; it is so essential that it may not be absent. This is the reason Gregory of Nazianzus refused a bishopric. Theophylact comments on this passage that 'this duty of teaching is above all others essential in those who are bishops.' Indeed, in the Councils of Nicea and Miletus, this was imposed instead of punishment, to hold the name of a minister, but not be allowed to preach the gospel.

2.   Authority, by which the preacher speaks as the ambassador of the great Jehovah (*Titus* 2:15; *1 Pet.* 4:11).

3.   Zeal, so that, in his longing for God's glory he will seek through his ministry to fulfil and effect the decree of God's election of men and women to salvation (*Job* 32:18, 19; *Col.* 1:28, 29; *2 Tim.* 2:25).

Physical Gestures

Gesture involves the action of either the voice or the body.

The voice ought to be loud enough for all to hear (*Isa.* 58:1; *John* 7:37; *Acts* 2:14). In the exposition of the doctrine in a sermon we ought to be more moderate, but in the exhortation more fervent and vehement. There should be a gravity about the gestures of the body which will in their own way grace the messenger of God. It is appropriate therefore, that the preacher keep the trunk of his body erect and still, while the other parts like the arm, the hand, the face and eyes may express and (as it were) speak the spiritual affections of his heart.

Scripture provides illustrations of the communicative

power of physical actions. The lifting up of the eye and the hand signifies confidence (*2 Chron.* 6:13, 14; *Acts* 7:55). The casting down of the eyes indicates sorrow and heaviness (*Luke* 18:13). As for gestures, we cannot lay down further principles; but here the example of widely respected godly ministers will serve as a guide.

11. *Public Prayer*

We have been considering the preaching of the Word. Now, finally, something should be said about leading in public prayer. This is the second aspect of prophesying. In it the minister is the voice of the people in calling upon God (*1 Sam.* 14:24; *Luke* 11:1).

In this connection we should note the following points:

1.   The subject of public prayer should be, first, the deficiencies and sins of the people, and then the graces of God and the blessings they stand in need of (*1 Tim.* 2:1, 2). Tertullian says, 'We do all pray for all emperors, that they may obtain a long life, a quiet reign, a safe family, courageous armies, a faithful council, loyal subjects, a peaceable world, and whatsoever things are desired of a man and of Caesar.' Again, 'We pray for emperors for their ministers and powers, for the state of the time, for the quietness of their affairs, and for the delaying of their death.' The Lord's Prayer covers these areas under six headings: God's glory, God's kingdom, and our obedience, the preservation of life, the forgiveness of sins, and the strengthening of the spirit.

2.   The form of prayer should be as follows: One voice, that of the minister alone, should lead in prayer, the congregation joining in silently but indicating their agreement at the end by saying, 'Amen' (*Neh.* 8:6; *Acts* 4:24;

1 Cor. 14:16). This was the practice in the early church, as Justin says: 'When the president has finished his prayers and thanksgivings, all the people present cry out with a favourable approbation, saying, Amen.'

3.   But the one voice which expresses the corporate prayers of the congregation needs to be understood (*1 Cor.* 14:15). It should not lead in prayer in a jagged and abrupt fashion, but with a steady flow of petitions, so that empty repetitions are avoided (*Matt.* 6:7).

4.   There are three elements in praying: (i) Carefully thinking about the appropriate content for prayer; (ii) Setting the themes in an appropriate order; (iii) Expressing the prayer so that it is made in public in a way that is edifying for the congregation.

To the Triune God be the glory!

Summary

Preaching involves·

1. Reading the text clearly from the canonical Scriptures.

2. Explaining the meaning of it, once it has been read, in the light of the Scriptures themselves.

3. Gathering a few profitable points of doctrine from the natural sense of the passage.

4. If the preacher is suitably gifted, applying the doctrines thus explained to the life and practice of the congregation in straightforward, plain speech.

The heart of the matter is this:

Preach one Christ,
by Christ,
to the praise of Christ.

Soli Deo Gloria
To God alone be the glory!

THE CALLING OF THE MINISTRY

I

Introduction

Job chapters 32 and 33 record a discussion between Elihu and Job. Elihu is portrayed as a dedicated, scholarly and able young man, and their conversation is centred on some of the most important and profound areas of theology. Chapter 33:1–7 serves as a preface to Elihu's speech. Then in verses 8–13 he repeats a number of Job's own propositions and criticises them; from there, to verses 32–33 he instructs Job on two particular issues in connection with God's dealing with sinners:

1. How God preserves a sinner from falling.
2. How God restores a sinner who has fallen.

Elihu argues that the means by which God preserves a sinner are twofold:

1. By warnings given in dreams and visions.
2. If these fail, then God employs scourges and chastisements.

These are expounded from verse 13 onwards. Then Elihu takes up his second point, the restoring of a sinner when these two means have not preserved him and, instead, he has fallen through his own corruption:

> If there be a messenger with him, or an interpreter, one of a thousand, to declare unto man his righteousness, Then will he have mercy upon him, and will say, Deliver him, that he go not down into the pit: for I have received a reconciliation.
>
> (*Job* 33:23–24, *Geneva Bible*)

In this connection he comments on:

1. The remedy and means of restoration.
2. The effect of such restoration.

The remedy is explained in verses 23 and 24. Then, in the rest of the chapter, the effects are described. When a sinner is restored by repentance, the graces of God for soul and body are poured out upon him.

So the point of this passage of Scripture is that in his mercy God uses means to preserve sinners from falling into sin. But if they fall, then in even greater mercy he provides means and helps to restore them. This is the sum and substance of the passage. Our concern here lies with these means and remedies.

The means God employs to restore a sinner after a fall is to raise him through repentance to a better condition than he was in before. That is inclusively and by implication taught in this text. But the instrument by whom this remarkable work is to be accomplished is clearly stated to be a minister of God, lawfully called and sent by him, and appointed by his church for such a great duty. Consequently these words contain a valuable description of a true minister. They describe him in five ways:

1. By his titles: he is 'a messenger', and 'an interpreter'.

2. By his rarity: he is 'one of a thousand'.

3. By his office: he is 'to declare . . . his righteousness'.

4. By the blessing that God gives to his labours: 'Then he will have mercy upon him'.

5. By his commission and authority in the last words God will say: 'Deliver him, that he go not down into the pit: for I have received a reconciliation.'

What follows is a brief survey of these marks of a true minister.

1. *The Titles of True Ministers*

Messenger

The first title of a minister of God is 'messenger', or 'angel'. This is his title here as well as in other Scriptures: 'He is the messenger of the Lord of hosts' (*Mal.* 2:7); in Revelation chapters 2 and 3 the ministers of the seven churches are called the angels of those churches. In one place a minister is an angel of God, and in the other place, the angel of the church, that is an angel, or messenger sent from God to his church.

This point has widespread application.

Firstly for ministers themselves. These pages are addressed largely to those who are either prophets, or sons of the prophets.[1] If you are a prophet, you are God's angel. If you are a son of the prophets you intend to be. You must understand your duty: prophets and ministers are angels; that is the very nature of their calling. Therefore you must preach God's Word, as God's Word, and deliver it just as you received it.

Angels, ambassadors and messengers do not carry their own message, but the message of the lords and masters who sent them. Similarly, ministers carry the message of the Lord of hosts, and are therefore bound to deliver it as the Lord's, not as their own.

[1] i.e. those who are engaged in the preaching ministry or are preparing for it.

The apostle Peter gives this exhortation: 'If anyone speaks, let him speak', not only the Word of God, but 'as the oracles of God' (*1 Pet.* 4:11). God's Word must be spoken, and it must be spoken *as* God's Word. We must show our faithfulness to the Lord in sincerely discharging the message which he has honoured us to carry. God's Word is pure. It must therefore be purely studied and delivered. Let all those who are God's angels – and desire to be honoured as his angels and ambassadors – fulfil the responsibilities of God's angels, lest (as many men mar a good tale in the telling) they take away the power and majesty of God's Word in the way they deliver it.

Secondly, if ministers are God's angels they must preach God's Word in a way that expresses and demonstrates the Spirit of God; for the Spirit of God must speak through God's angel.

To preach in the demonstration of God's Spirit is to preach with such plainness, and yet with such power, that even the least intellectually gifted recognise that it is not man but God himself who is teaching them. Yet at the same time, the conscience of the mightiest may feel not man but God reproving them through the power of the Spirit. This is clear from Paul's words: 'But if all prophesy, and an unbeliever or an uninformed person comes in, he is convinced by all, he is convicted by all. And thus the secrets of his heart are revealed; and so, falling down on his face, he will worship God and report that God is truly among you' (*1 Cor.* 14:24, 25).

Notice the plainness and the power of which these words speak (although one might think that these two things could hardly belong together).

Notice the plainness. Since even the uneducated person sees his faults revealed, it follows that he understands what is said; and if he can understand it, then it must be plain. Then, in addition, notice the power: his conscience is so convinced, his secret faults so unveiled, and his heart so ripped up that he says, 'Certainly God speaks in this man'.

This is the real evidence and proof of God's Spirit. It is taken as high commendation in the world's eyes when men say of a preacher, 'He is a real scholar', because he is scholarly, well-read, has a retentive memory and a good delivery. So it is, and such commendation (if deserved) should not be despised. But what commends a man to the Lord his God and to his own conscience is that he preaches with a plainness suited to the ability, and so powerfully to the conscience, of a wicked man that he realises that God is present in the preacher.

Are you an angel of God? Then magnify the Spirit of God, and not yourself, in your preaching of his Word.

Thirdly, there is also an important application to hearers. They are taught here that if their ministers are angels sent to them from God, then they should hear them gladly, willingly, reverently and obediently. Gladly and willingly because they are ambassadors; reverently and obediently because they are sent from the high God, the King of kings, and it is his message they deliver.

God says, 'People should seek the law from his mouth' (*Mal.* 2:7). And with good reason, for if the law is the revealed will of God, and the minister is the angel of God, then where should they seek the will of God but at the mouth of his angel? Such is the logic of this text: we should 'seek the law at his mouth, for he is the messenger of the Lord of hosts'. All Christians must do this, not only when the doctrine that is preached pleases us, but also when it cuts across our corruption, and is completely contrary to our dispositions. It may be highly distasteful and hurt our natural desires. But since it is a message from our God and King, and the teacher is the angel or messenger of that God, both he and it must be received with respect, and with an obedience that comes from our hearts and souls.

This is the reason why respect and honour should be given by all genuine Christians to God's ministers (especially when they adorn their high calling with a holy life): they are angels of God. St Paul says that 'the woman ought to have a symbol of authority on her head, because of the angels' (*1 Cor.* 11:10). But not only because the holy angels are present, and always behold our service of God; ministers who are angels and messengers sent from God are there, delivering the message and charge they have received from God.

Interpreter

The minister of the gospel is also an interpreter. He is someone who is able to deliver the reconciliation made between God and man. I do not mean that he is the author of reconciliation; that is the Godhead alone. Nor is he the effecter of this reconciliation; that is the second person, Christ Jesus. Nor is he the assurer or ratifier of it; that is the Holy Spirit. Nor is he the instrument of it; that is the good news of the gospel. But he *is* the interpreter of it.

First of all he is someone who can expound and explain the covenant of grace, and rightly lay down how this reconciliation is accomplished. Secondly, he is someone who can properly and accurately apply the means for its outworking. Thirdly, he is someone who has authority to proclaim and declare it when it is effected. In these three ways he is God's interpreter to the people.

But he is also the people's interpreter to God. He is able to speak to God on their behalf, to lay bare their need and vulnerability, to confess their sins, to pray for pardon and forgiveness, and to give thanks on their behalf for the mercies they have received. In a word, he can offer up for them all their spiritual sacrifices to God.

Thus every true minister is a dual interpreter: he is both God's interpreter to the people, and the people's to God. In these respects he is properly called God's mouth to the people (by preaching to them from God), and the people's mouth to God (by praying for them to God). This underlines what a great and glorious calling the ministry is, if it is rightly understood.

What are the practical implications of this?

First, if every true minister must be God's interpreter to the people, and the people's to God, then every one who either is or intends to be a minister must have the 'tongue of the learned' (*Isa.* 50:4). There the prophet says (first in the name of Christ, the great prophet and teacher of his church, and secondly in his own name and that of all true prophets there will ever be): 'The Lord God has given Me the tongue of the learned, That I should know to speak a word in season to him who is weary.' The weary soul or troubled conscience must have a word in season spoken to him for his comfort. This cannot be done without 'the tongue of the learned'. And the 'tongue of the learned' must be given by God.

To possess the 'tongue of the learned', of which Isaiah speaks, is to be the interpreter which the Holy Spirit here says a minister must be. To be able to speak with this tongue is to possess three things (i) Human learning; (ii) Divine knowledge insofar as that may be learned from others; (iii) In addition, whoever speaks with this tongue must be inwardly taught and instructed by the Spirit of God. The first two can be learned from men, but the third only from God; a true minister must be inwardly taught by the spiritual schoolmaster, the Holy Spirit.

In Revelation, John receives from Christ. He must take the book, that is the Scripture, and eat it. Then, when he has eaten it (says the angel) he must go to preach to 'peoples, nations, tongues, and kings' (*Rev.* 10:8–11). John did, of course, eat the book. This was fulfilled, fundamentally, in the coming down of the Holy Spirit, the very purpose of whose coming was to teach them spiritually (see *Acts* 2). But, through John, Christ teaches his church in a permanent way that ministers are not fit to preach to nations and to kings until they have eaten the book of God; that is, until above and beyond all the learning that man can impart, they are also taught by the Spirit of God himself.

It is this teaching that makes a man a true interpreter. Without it he cannot be one. How can anyone be God's interpreter to his people unless he knows the mind of God himself? And how can he know the mind of God except by the teaching of the Spirit of God? As no man knows the thoughts of a man but the spirit of man that is in him, so the things of God are known by no man but only by the Spirit of God (*1 Cor.* 2:11).

We can learn to interpret human writing by human learning, and even interpret the Scriptures truly and soundly as a human book or story, in such a way as to increase knowledge; but the divine and spiritual interpreter, who pierces the heart and takes men's souls by surprise, must be taught by the inward teaching of the Holy Spirit.

I am not here making any allowance for the claims people make that they have received 'revelations'. These have no substance; they are either dreams of their own, or illusions of the devil. They despise both human learning and the study of the Scriptures, and trust exclusively in 'revelations of the Spirit'. But God's Spirit does not work except on the foundation of the Word.

What I am stressing is this: a minister must be a divine interpreter, an interpreter of God's meaning. And therefore he must not only read the book, but eat it. He must not only have the knowledge of divine things flowing in his brain, but engraved on his heart and printed in his soul by the spiritual finger of God. To this end, after all his own study, meditation and discussion, his use of commentaries and other human helps, he must pray with David, 'Open my eyes, that I may see wondrous things from Your law' (*Psa.* 119:18).

Recognising these wonders requires spiritual illumination, and the exposition of them requires the tongue of the learned. Consequently, after all the study which flesh and blood and human reason can yield, we need to pray with the prophet, 'Lord, give me the tongue of the learned, that I may be a right interpreter of your holy will.'

Furthermore since ministers are interpreters, they must strive for sanctification and holiness in their own lives. In Isaiah, the kingdom of Assyria is said to be sanctified, or set apart, to destroy God's enemies. If there is a certain kind of sanctification necessary for the work of destruction, how much more is true sanctification necessary for the great and glorious work of the edification of God's church?

A minister is to declare the reconciliation between God and man. If he himself is not reconciled, dare he present another man to God's mercy for pardon when he has never presented himself? Can he commend the state of grace to another without ever having felt the sweetness of it in his own soul? Dare he preach on sanctification with polluted lips, and out of an unsanctified heart?

Moses was not allowed to stand on the mount in God's presence until he had taken his shoes off his feet (*Exod.* 3:5). How then can anyone presume to come into the most high and holy presence of the Lord, until he has put his own corruptions to death and thrown aside his unruly affections?

In Exodus, the priests are commanded to sanctify the people, and in Leviticus 10:3 it is said that God will be sanctified in all who come near to him. But who comes as near to him as ministers do? So it is clear that ministers sanctify the people, and in a sense, God himself. Shall they in one sense be sanctifiers of the people, but in no sense sanctifiers of themselves? If that is so, they are lame interpreters indeed. This is undoubtedly the reason why the work of unsanctified ministers and of those with a careless life-style bears so little fruit in the church.

Many ministers have no lack of learning or of ability to interpret the Scriptures; yet how many people do they bring to God? Some are converted by their ministry, but even this may happen so that God can show that the power of the gospel is not in the person who preaches it, but in his own ordinance. But there are few such converts (as far as we can see), and this teaches us that God hates anyone who takes it in hand to reconcile others to God while he himself remains unreconciled.

Since ministers are God's interpreters to the people, to declare their reconciliation with God; and since they cannot be reconciled unless they are also sanctified; since the people can hardly be sanctified by the ministry of an unsanctified man, let all true ministers of God first of all be God's interpreters to their own consciences, and be their own souls' interpreters to God. Then they will know better how to discharge the office of true interpreters between God and his people.

2. *The Scarcity of True Ministers*

The text in Job 33 continues by describing the messenger as 'one of a thousand'. Here, in the second part of the description, emphasis is placed on the scarcity or rarity of good ministers. This is underlined by a very unusual phrase. A true minister, one who is a genuine angel and a true interpreter is no common or ordinary man. Such men are thin on the ground, one of many – indeed, 'one of a thousand'.

This can be taken either literally or figuratively. In the figurative sense, it is true of ministers in and of them-selves; in the strict, literal sense, the comparison is with all men. According to the figurative, hyperbolical sense: among all ministers, not one of many is a right angel and a true interpreter. According to the plain and literal sense: among the men of this world, there is not one in a thousand who proves to be a true minister.

We should note three things in connection with this statement: the truth of it, the reasons for it, and the application of it.

The truth of it is self-evident from the experience of all ages. It is strange, but true, that few men of any sort, especially men of quality, seek the calling of a minister. What is even stranger is how few of those who have the title 'minister' deserve the honourable names of an angel and an interpreter. The truth is too obvious in ordinary experience to need spelling out. Instead, let us see the reasons for this situation. They are principally as follows:

First, the contempt with which the calling is treated. It is always hated by wicked and irreverent men because it reveals their filthiness and unmasks their hypocrisy. The teaching of ministers is frequently a fretting corrosive on their conscience, preventing them from weltering and wallowing quietly and secretly in their sins – as they would be able to do under other circumstances. This is why they spurn both the calling of ministers and ministers themselves. They watch them carefully to latch onto their smallest failures, hoping to disgrace them. They imagine that by casting contempt on the calling of the preacher they can remove the shame from their own degraded ways.

It is inevitable that they should hate those who are called to the ministry, since they harbour a deadly hatred both for the law and for the gospel message which they bring, and for the God whose representatives they are. It was experiencing this hatred and disgrace in a wicked world that caused Jeremiah to cry, 'Woe is me,' and made him, from his own human perspective, 'curse the time that ever he was a prophet'. He says, 'I am a man of contention' (*Jer.* 15:10). It seemed that every man was in conflict and at enmity with him.

The second reason is the difficulty of discharging the duties of a minister's calling. To stand in God's presence, to enter into the holy of holies, to go between God and his people, to be God's mouth to his people, and the people's to God; to be the interpreter of the eternal law of the Old Testament and the everlasting gospel of the New; to stand in the place and even bear the office of Christ himself, to take the care and charge of souls – these considerations overwhelm the consciences of men who approach the sacred seat of the preacher with reverence and not with rashness.

It was this that made the apostle Paul cry out, 'Who is sufficient for these things?' (*2 Cor.* 2:16). And if Paul said, 'Who is sufficient?' it is no surprise that many others say, 'I am not sufficient,' and therefore remove their necks from this yoke and their hands from this plough, until either God himself, or his church, presses them into it.

The third and last reason is especially relevant to ministry in the New Testament era, namely the inadequacy of the financial recompense and status given to those who enter this calling.

All men are flesh and blood. In that respect they must be allured and won to embrace this vocation by the kind of arguments which may well persuade flesh and blood. The world has had a careless attitude about this in every age. Consequently in the law, God gave careful instructions for the maintenance of the Levites (*Num.* 18:26). But especially now, under the gospel, the ministerial calling is poorly provided for, even although it deserves to be rewarded most of all. Certainly it would be an honourable Christian policy to make at least good provision for this calling, so that men of the worthiest gifts might be won for it.

The lack of such provision is the reason why so many young men with unusual ability and great prospects turn to other vocations, especially law. That is where most of the sharpest minds in our nation are employed. Why? Because in legal practice they have all the means for their advance, whereas the ministry, generally speaking, yields nothing but a clear road to poverty.

This is a great blemish on our church. I wish it were not true that the Roman Catholics, those children of this world, are wiser (in this particular area), than the church of God. Reformation here is a work worth the labour of both prince and people.

Unless special attention is given to this matter, it will be left unreformed. No doubt, in the Old Testament period, if God himself had not given direct orders for the material support of the Levites, they would have suffered the same privation as the ministry does today. These considerations, taken together, produce an infallible argument. For who will accept such vile contempt and such a weighty responsibility for no reward? But where there is so much contempt and such a heavy burden, yet such a poor reward, is it any wonder that a good minister is one in a thousand?

Now we must apply this teaching. In fact it leads to manifold applications and provides directions for a variety of people:

First, rulers and magistrates are taught here that if good ministers are so scarce, in order to maintain and increase them, they must do all they can for the 'schools of the prophets', those universities, colleges and schools providing true learning which are the seminaries for the ministry.

Samuel's example is worthy of imitation. The schools of the prophets flourished in his day. Saul did much damage in Israel, but when he came to the schools of the prophets, even his hard heart relented. He could do them no harm, indeed, he put off his robes and prophesied amongst them (*1 Sam.* 19:20–24). In the same way all Christian rulers and magistrates should promote the cause of their schools, and see that they are both well maintained and well provided for. This is an obvious and a weighty conclusion.

Good ministers are one in a thousand. If therefore their number is to be increased, training institutions must be well maintained. In order to uphold the kingdom of Satan, Antichrist is careful to erect colleges and endow them with financial backing, to be seminaries for his synagogue (Rome, Rheims, Douai and so on).[1] He employs strenuous means to sow his tares in the hearts of young men, so that they may in turn sow them in the hearts of people abroad. Should not Christian rulers be just as careful, indeed, even more zealous, to increase the number of godly ministers? Shall Baal have his 400 prophets, and God have only his Elijah (*1 Kings* 18:22)? Shame on Ahab, or on any king, whose kingdom is in that state.

The Jesuits' diligence is such in teaching, and the readiness of some of their novices such in learning (the devil himself doubtless providing help), that in three years (as some of them say of themselves) they make considerable advance in human learning, and in the fourth, in theology. If this is so, then it may be a good lesson for our own schools of learning, and an inducement to persuade those who govern them to labour to encourage learning by every appropriate means, and to speed its advance. This would put to shame some who spend many years in the universities but, despite that, never prove to be 'one of a thousand'.

By God's mercy, in our schools many young trees have been planted by the riverside of this godly orchard. By careful tending and dressing they may prove to be good trees in the temple of God and strong pillars in the church. But they are like tender plants, and must be cherished. Rulers and men of standing, by providing for maintenance, and the governors of our schools by establishing good order and being concerned about their task, must see that these plants have sufficient moisture

---

[1] Perkins is referring here to the centres of learning which strengthened the Roman Catholic Counter-Reformation. From Douai and Rheims carefully trained priests spread to various parts of Europe to defend and promulgate Roman Catholicism.

to grow speedily to full maturity. Then they must see to it that at the right time they are transplanted into the church and commonwealth.

These are the trees spoken of in Ezekiel 47:7 which grow by the sides of the river which flowed out of the sanctuary. Water from the sanctuary must nourish them, so that they grow up to their full height. But take away these waters, take away the liberality of rulers, and good discipline from the universities, and these trees will inevitably decay and wither. If they do, then the small number of good ministers will be even smaller, and from being 'one of a thousand', there will not even be one in two thousand.

Secondly, ministers themselves are taught these lessons:

1. If good ministers are so scarce, we must take great care not to decrease their number. Every man must therefore labour first for the ability, and then for the conscientiousness to discharge his duty; namely to be an angel, to deliver faithfully God's message, and to be a true interpreter standing between God and his people. If you do, even although the number of good ministers is small, you will not make it any smaller.

2. If ministers are few in number, then do all you can to increase their number. The greater the number, the lighter the burden lying on each individual man. So, let every minister both in his teaching and his conversation work in such a way that he honours his calling, so that he may attract others to share his love for it.

3. Are good ministers too thinly sown on the ground? Are there all too few of them? Then let all good and godly ministers give the right hand of fellowship to each other (*Gal.* 2:9) and unite together in love. In this way they will

arm themselves against the scorn and contempt of the world.

Those who belong to a family, or a brotherhood, or any kind of society, know that the fewer they are in number, the more closely they will combine resources and the more firmly they will unite against a foreign force. God's ministers ought to do the same, because they are so small in numbers. If they were numerous, there would be less danger in their division. But since they are so few, it is all the more important for them to avoid divisions, and all occasions of debate, and to join hands against common adversaries.

In the third place, young students are here taught – since a true minister is but 'one of a thousand' – to direct both their studies and their thoughts to the ministry. Remember the old proverb: 'The best things are hard to come by.'

It is undoubtedly true that there are so few good ministers because the holy ministry is such a high and excellent calling. But while it is disgraceful that there are so few good ministers, it is also a commendation of the calling. Such is its honour and excellency that, since scarcely one in a thousand attains to it, only men of the most outstanding gifts are here invited to dedicate themselves to this most excellent vocation. Yes, reason itself would urge a man to be 'one of a thousand'!

Furthermore, as students aspire to this rare and excellent calling, they must learn to equip themselves with the best helps and means they can, in order to become true ministers and able interpreters. They must not delay too long in those studies which keep a man from the practice of this high office. For the calling is not to live in the university or in the college and to study, however eager an individual is to devour learning. It is, rather, to be a good minister. That is what makes a man 'one of a thousand'.

Fourthly, those who listen to the preaching of their ministers are also taught what their duty is. It is, first of all, to respect them and respectfully to receive the message of every true messenger, because it is such a rare thing to find a true minister. Nothing is worse or more despicable than evil and immoral ministers. Christ himself compares them to salt which has lost its savour – good for nothing but to be thrown out, and trampled down by men (*Matt.* 5:13). In the same way, no-one is worthy of more love and reverence than a holy minister. As Isaiah says, even the feet of those who bring glad tidings are beautiful (*Isa.* 52:7). We should kiss the feet of those who bring news of peace. Christians should, therefore, receive and treat a good minister as Paul says the Galatians formerly treated him: 'as an angel of God' (*Gal.* 4:14).

Do you have a godly pastor? Confer with him. Go to him for comfort and counsel; profit from his company, sit under his ministry frequently; count him worthy of 'double honour' (*1 Tim.* 5:17). Never imagine that it is a small or commonplace blessing to have 'one of a thousand'. Thank God for giving this mercy to you, which he has denied to so many others. For some have no minister while others have a minister, who, alas, is not 'one of a thousand'.

Furthermore, those who are fathers should learn to consecrate their children to God for the work of the ministry, since it is such an uncommon and glorious thing to be a good minister. Any man can count himself happy and honoured by God if he is the father of a son who proves to be 'one of a thousand'.

To conclude this point briefly, since good ministers are

so scarce, we must all learn 'to pray the Lord of the harvest, to send out labourers into His harvest' (*Matt.* 9:38). We must pray too for those who are already called, that God would make them faithful in their high office. Let us pray as Elisha did when he asked Elijah that the good spirit would be doubled on him (*2 Kings* 2:9), so that the number may be increased. For a good minister is 'one of a thousand'.

3. *The Office of True Ministers*

This statement in Job continues with a third element in the description of a minister. It is his task 'to declare unto man his righteousness'.

He is to do this when a poor sinner is, as it were, brought down to the very gates of hell by his sins (when he sees how foul they are and feels the burden they bring). When this sinner, by the preaching of the law, is brought to a true sight of his misery; and then, by the preaching of the gospel, is brought to lay hold on Jesus Christ, then it is the proper office of a minister 'to declare unto that man his righteousness'.

Although in himself he is as sick and foul as sin can make him, and as the law can show him to be, in Christ he is righteous and just. Indeed, he is so justified by Christ that he is no longer a sinner in God's presence or in his reckoning.

This is the righteousness a Christian has; this is the justification of a sinner. To declare this righteousness to those who repent and believe is the proper duty of a true minister.

In Acts, Paul says of himself that he witnessed to the Jews and to the Gentiles, 'repentance toward God and faith toward our Lord Jesus Christ' (*Acts* 20:21). These words summarise the complete duty of a minister as a public angel or interpreter. First, he is to preach the repentance which we must express to God, whom we have grievously offended by our sins. Secondly, he is to preach faith in Christ, and free forgiveness, and perfect salvation through that faith in Christ, to all who truly believe in him. And afterwards he does what is described here, which includes both of these things; namely, 'to declare unto man his righteousness'. Thus, we find the following elements in a minister's calling are underlined:

Firstly, a true minister may – indeed must – tell sinners where righteousness is to be found, namely in Jesus Christ the righteous.

Secondly, he will make clear *how* that righteousness may be obtained, namely by fulfilling two duties:

1. By denying and rejecting his own righteousness, which is done by repentance.

2. By claiming and clinging to Christ's righteousness, which is done by faith.

Thirdly, a true minister may and must declare this righteousness to his hearers. This means that he will:

1. Explain and proclaim that this righteousness is waiting to be granted to every sinner who will take hold of it, and that it is able to justify and save him.

2. Over and above making known the message of justification, he must (as Paul did) witness and testify to the conscience of the sinner, that this message is as true as God himself is true.

When we are in doubt about the truth of a situation we call on a witness whose testimony may clear up the truth. In a similar way, the consciences of poor sinners waver and are uncertain what to believe when they have doubts about this righteousness. Then the true minister is to act as God's faithful witness to the doubting and distressed conscience, to bear witness to and affirm the truth, from his own conscience, knowledge and feeling of the infallible certainty of God's promises.

3.   If the sinner's conscience is not yet pacified, the minister must maintain this truth and righteousness against all who deny it, against the powers of darkness and all the gates of hell. He must assert that the gospel brings true and perfect righteousness to whoever receives it in the way indicated. This is infallibly the case for every one who repents and believes. Thus the minister may assure the conscience of the sinner from the Word of truth and in the name of God, and may call to witness all God's saints and all his holy angels. He may well pledge his own soul on the fact that this is a true, perfect and all-sufficient righteousness.

This, in some measure, is what it means 'to declare unto man his righteousness'. This is the special office of a minister of God, and the greatest and finest aspect of his work.

When there is a lack of godly ministers, godly Christian men can still profitably help one another to do these things. That notwithstanding, this privilege is the proper function of a godly minister. The promise and blessing belong properly to him; as the consciences of all penitent sinners will testify.

David is an example. Through Nathan's preaching, he was cast down to the very mouth of hell by the terrible realisation of his two hideous sins. But when in faith he began to wrestle against hell, and strive against despair, and to lay hold of the mercy of God in Christ, not even the testimony of all the men in the world could have given him the joy, comfort, and assurance that Nathan did, when he said – as a prophet and a true minister – 'The Lord also has put away your sin; you shall not die' (*2 Sam.* 12:13). What was Nathan doing here but the duty of every true minister?

If this is the office and duty of a minister and if this is the glory of his office, then a number of important implications follow.

In relation to the ministry, it first shows how inadequate it is for the Roman Catholic Church to assure people of their righteousness when they let them seek it in themselves, where, alas, it can never be found. Paul himself testifies to his desire to be found out of himself, and in Christ (*Phil.* 3:9). Yet if ever a man had righteousness of his own worth trusting in, Paul was that man.

This is the reason why so many Roman Catholics never find that righteousness which will calm and satisfy their consciences when they come to die. It also explains why so many of them, when it comes to the issue, abandon their own resources, and, like ourselves, seek for this righteousness in Christ. In him it is both assuredly and sufficiently found.

Several things can also be learned, positively, for our own ministry.

First, the true way to teach and declare righteousness. This is not preaching either the law alone, or the gospel alone, as some unwisely do, with the result that both are preached without profit. Both the law and the gospel must be preached; the law to give birth to repentance and the gospel to lead to faith. But they must be preached in their proper order, first the law to bring repentance and then the gospel to work faith and forgiveness – never the other way round.

Secondly, ministers are taught to be holy, sanctified and reconciled themselves. Can it be your duty to declare to others their righteousness, yet not declare your own righteousness to yourself? How can you be a true witness to testify between God and sinners, if you yourself neither know nor feel the truth of your testimony?

David says to the sinner, 'I will instruct you and teach

you in the way you should go' (*Psa.* 32:8). But in the same psalm he first of all sets down his own experience in an extended description of his repentance and of God's mercy on himself.

God sometimes does satisfy and save a poor distressed sinner by the testimony of such men, to teach us that the power to do so lies in the truth of his covenant and not in the man. There are all too few to teach us how much it pleases God when a minister declares the righteousness to others which he possesses first himself and witnesses to others about a truth which he first knows in his own experience.

Thirdly, a sense of the high privilege of their calling strengthens all true ministers in the face of the scorn and contempt of the world which wicked men throw in their faces like dust and mud. They can be content with this: they are the men God has called to declare the gift of righteousness. Even those who scorn and despise the ministry can possess righteousness only by means of a poor minister! So do your duty, and those who mock you will have cause to honour you.

This should encourage students to consecrate themselves to the ministry. What calling has as great a responsibility as this, 'to declare unto man his righteousness'? Of course in this perverse world you are undervalued (if it highly valued you it would not be so perverse!). But you are honoured in the hearts of all God's children, and even in the consciences of some who malign you. Thousands, when they die, will bless you, who earlier in their lives were indifferent to you. The devil himself envies you, and even the holy angels admire the honour of your calling because you have power 'to declare unto man his righteousness'.

In relation to those who hear the gospel preached. If anyone is to receive this righteousness in Christ for himself he must seek it where it can be found, namely in both the law and the gospel; not in the gospel alone; but first in the law, and then the gospel. We must never try to taste the sweetness of the gospel when we have not first swallowed the bitter pill of the law. If, therefore, we want to be declared righteous by the gospel, we must be content first to be pronounced miserable by the law. If we want to be declared righteous in Christ, then we must be content first to be pronounced sinful and unrighteous in ourselves.

In addition, we are taught here to value the ministers of God. These words show us the appropriate reverence and obedience we owe them and their teaching, since they are the ones who proclaim righteousness to us, if we have any.

If you were to lose a precious jewel that was your only valuable possession, would you not feel deeply indebted to anyone who could tell you where it was and help you to find it? Or to a lawyer who would defend you in a law court, or to a physician who helped you to recover your health? Surely, then, you are indebted to a godly minister who, when Adam had lost the jewel of righteousness (the wealth of your soul as well as his own), can truly tell you where it is, and how it can be recovered; who, when the devil hauls you to the bar of God's justice, to be tried for your sins, can win such a verdict that even the devil himself cannot overturn it; and who, when your soul is terminally ill and liable to damnation, can heal its deadly wounds. A good minister, whose task it is to 'declare unto man his righteousness' is, as Paul says, worthy of 'double honour'.

One final point will conclude this chapter: the high honour of the ministerial office should encourage fathers to dedicate their sons to such a holy calling. The physician's care for your body, or the lawyer's for your court case, are both inferior services to that of the minister. One in ten may be a good lawyer; one in twenty a good physician; one in a hundred may be a good man; but a good minister is one in a thousand! A good lawyer can explain the exact standing of your case; a physician can explain the truth about your physical condition. But no other calling, no other man, can tell you about your righteousness; only a true minister can do that.

So much, then, for the office or function of a minister. Now we must turn to consider the blessing which follows his work.

4. *The Blessing of the Work of True Ministers*

The fourth aspect of this description of a true minister is the blessing which God bestows on his work and service. 'Then' – when by the preaching of the law someone is brought to true humiliation and repentance, and by the preaching of the gospel to true faith in the Messiah – 'then will he [God] have mercy on him [the penitent and believing sinner]'.

Notice the sympathy and co-operation there is between the heart of God and the task of the minister. Man preaches and God blesses; man works on the heart and God gives grace; the minister expounds righteousness and God says, 'So be it, he shall be righteous'; a minister pronounces mercy to a penitent sinner and immediately God has mercy on him.

Here we see the great and glorious estimate God has of the Word his ministers preach, when it is truly taught and properly applied. It is as though he ties his blessing to it. Ordinarily until someone knows this righteousness by means of an interpreter, God does not have mercy on him, but as soon as he does know it, then as we see here, 'God will have mercy on him, and will say, "Deliver him."'

It is a considerable honour for ministers and for their ministry that God himself blesses it, and works when they work. He waits patiently while they declare his righteousness and 'then he has mercy on him'. The word spoken by a minister of God is as powerful as that.

This is simply what Christ promised: 'Whatever you loose on earth will be loosed in heaven' (*Matt.* 16:19). If we want to know what this means, John's Gospel gives us the answer: 'If you forgive the sins of any, they are forgiven them; if you retain the sins of any, they are retained' (*John* 20:23). If we want to know what this means, Isaiah explains it: 'Who frustrates the signs of the babblers, And drives diviners mad; Who turns wise men backward, and makes their knowledge foolishness; Who confirms the word of His servant, and performs the counsel of His messengers' (*Isa.* 44:25–26). In this way, God binds and looses with ministers and remits and retains with them, by confirming their word and fulfilling their warnings.

For example, a true minister may see a sinner hardened in his sins and still rebelling against the will of God. He therefore declares his unrighteousness and sins and warns of the just misery and divine condemnation which he merits. Here he binds on earth, here he retains on earth; there, in heaven, this man's sins are likewise bound or retained.

On the other hand, the true minister may see someone who is penitent and believing and assure him of the forgiveness of sins and real happiness. He thus frees him from the bondage of his sins by telling him he is now righteous. This person's sins are likewise loosed and remitted in heaven. God himself pronounces him free in heaven when the minister does on earth. Thus God 'confirms the word of His servant, and performs the counsel of His messengers'.

Several applications of this should be noted:

First this teaches rulers and others in positions of authority to be nursing fathers and mothers to the church, because their authority over them is such that what they decree is confirmed in heaven. They hold influential positions and are described in Scripture as 'gods' on earth (*Psa.* 82:1, 6). Yet they must acknowledge that in justifying a sinner, in the message they interpret, in their declaration of righteousness, in their binding and loosing, the power ministers of the gospel have comes directly from God and is above their own. So they themselves, as individuals, must submit to the powerful word of ministers, to be taught by it, and to be reconciled by means of it. They must learn to respect it, for even although it is a man who speaks, it is still the Word of God.

This is what it means to lick the dust of Christ's feet, as Isaiah puts it (*Isa.* 49:23). It is far from what the Pope suggests it is: to hold the stirrup, and lead the horse, to hold the water to the Pope, to kiss his toes, to hold a kingdom from him like a tenant, at his will or by his courtesy. Instead it is reverently to acknowledge that it is God who has ordained the ministry and that its function and task are high and noble. It is to acknowledge that the power of ministers' keys and censures (when they are rightly applied), their promises and their warnings, come from God, and to submit to them.

Secondly, ministers themselves must remember, when they take the word of reconciliation into their hands and mouths, whose it is. It is exclusively the Lord's. They must recall that he works with them, therefore they must use it in a holy manner, in fear and reverence. It is not their own word; they may not use it in any way they please.

Thirdly, those who listen to preaching are taught, first, to see how foolish it is to do so either rarely or carelessly, while they consult wizards and charmers instead. They are simply the devil's prophets.

Consider the difference between these two: the wizard and charmer has his fellowship with the devil, the preacher with God; the charmer has his calling from the devil, the preacher has his from God. The charmer's charm is the devil's watchword – when he charms, the devil does the feat; but the preacher's doctrine is God's watchword – when he truly applies it, God himself ratifies and confirms it.

So we must fear to have anything to do with the devil in this way, seeking guidance from those who are his slaves. Instead, let us draw near to God, by entering into fellowship with his holy prophets and godly ministers.

Furthermore, when they preach and you believe, 'and God have mercy on you', you should realise the respect they and their word deserve since it has been accompanied by God's mercy and forgiveness. Learn, too, to hear the Word of God with 'fear and trembling' (*Phil.* 2:12), because it is God's Word, and not theirs. When a true minister says, with good reason, 'I denounce you as a sinful man, and under the curse,' or 'I declare you to be righteous and a child of grace,' that is just as solemn as if God himself had spoken to you from heaven.

But surely it is just as good if someone who is not a minister pronounces forgiveness for me when I repent? Undoubtedly this is the case in extraordinary times or places, when there are no ministers. But in every other context this blessing is principally tied to the minister's calling. Scripture nowhere speaks of this as the calling of a private individual, in the way it speaks of it here in relationship to ministers: 'If there be a messenger with him, or an interpreter, one of a thousand, to declare unto man his righteousness, Then will he have mercy upon him, and will say, "Deliver him."'

What is the source of such a blessing? It comes from this promise of God. If other callings were to claim to give the same blessing, they would need to have the same promise. Besides, other Christians may be sanctified as individuals, and have a good measure of knowledge, yet they do not possess the same spiritual discernment as godly ministers. Nor are they so fully and truly able to judge when someone has genuinely repented. Consequently they cannot so reliably pronounce the sentence of the law or the gospel. Nor, ordinarily, is their conversation and Christian counsel as instrumental in conversion as it is in encouraging those who have already been converted. That power normally belongs to the public ministry of the Word. Ordinarily, therefore, Christians in general do not have the power to pronounce the sentence of binding or loosing on anyone.

I admit that, if there is no minister, God blesses the labours of private individuals who have knowledge, sometimes in conversion as well as in bringing comfort at the hour of death. On such occasions God gives a strength and power to the promise they give to someone who is penitent. But these are unusual circumstances when there are no ministers. In these circumstances a knowledgeable and godly individual becomes a minister either to himself or to someone else.

There is a parallel situation in civic life. In a situation of extreme danger when there is no magistrate present, a private individual becomes a magistrate himself to defend his own life. Under these circumstances, the sword of the magistrate is put into the hands of a private individual. In the same way, when there are no ministers, the authority of the ministry is committed to the hands of private men (in days of persecution for example). At such a time they may give comforting admonition and advice as well as authoritatively pronounce mercy and forgiveness to one another when there is true repentance.

But remember that in these circumstances a private

man acts as a minister during that time and in this circumstance only. Normally (*always* in settled churches) this power is part of the work of the ministry alone. This is implied in ordination. To the minister belongs the promise and the blessing that when he has 'declared to a man his righteousness, then God will have mercy on him'.

5. The Commission and Authority of True Ministers

Elihu's statement continues: '. . . and will say, "Deliver him, that he go not down into the pit: for I have received a reconciliation."'

The fifth and last part of this description of the gospel minister is the commission and authority given to him. It is greater than that given to any other creature. It amounts to this: when a minister of God has declared someone to be righteous and has brought him to the state of grace, and God in his favour has had mercy on him, then God says to the minister: 'Deliver that soul from hell, for I have pardoned him in Christ. I am reconciled to him.'

In these words the minister of God is given authority to redeem the penitent individual from hell and from damnation. Of course, the minister is not the means of working out this redemption. That belongs totally and exclusively to Christ himself. But the minister is God's instrument and Christ's instrument – first, to apply the means of reconciliation; and second, to pronounce the individual to be safe and delivered when these means are used.

This is the greatest honour of all in the call to the ministry. In fact it is the greatest privilege given to either man or angel because it is clearly a commission to go and deliver people from the power of hell, to redeem them to be God's children, and to make them heirs of heaven. The angels of heaven have never had this commission. They are messengers sent out for the good of those whom ministers have redeemed (*Heb.* 1:14), They have brought many comfortable messages to them. But no heavenly angel was ever told, 'Deliver that man from going down to the pit,' as is said here to a minister. Only ministers have this commission.

In relation to some callings God says, 'Work for man, build him houses, provide him sustenance.' To the physician he says, 'Heal that man'; to the lawyer: 'Do that man justice'; to the soldier: 'Fight for him'; to the magistrate: 'Defend him'; to the king: 'Govern him, and see that everyone does his duty'. But it is only to the minister that God says: 'Deliver him from going down to the pit.'

If this is the case, then these applications follow:

First, ministers must learn that if they are to have the honour of redeemers they must do the work of redeemers. They must pray earnestly for the people, which is one means by which they redeem men. They must learn to say with Samuel, 'Far be it from me that I should sin against the Lord in ceasing to pray for you' (*1 Sam.* 12:23). They must learn to mourn for the impenitent, when they refuse to turn to God. David did. His eyes gushed out with rivers of water, because men did not keep God's law (*Psa.* 119:136). Similarly, Jeremiah wished there were a fountain of waters in his eyes so that he might weep for the sins of the people (*Jer.* 9:1).

Ministers must confer with their people and also visit, admonish and rebuke them in private. Most of all they must preach, and do so in such a manner and with such diligence that they may redeem souls. Winning souls is the goal they must have in view.

Some preach out of a fear of the law, to avoid criticism or punishment; others preach because it is fashionable, in order to be like others; some do it for show, to win credit and praise; others do it out of ambition, to rise in the world. But if they do they are forgetting their commission, which is: *Deliver a man from hell.* This should be the aim of their preaching. What should commissioners do, but fulfil their commission? High commissioners deserve to become low commissioners, or rather not commissioners at all, if they do not fulfil their duties. It is therefore tragic to see how some by not preaching and others by their vain preaching, show that they intend anything but winning souls for God.

So then, all faithful ministers preach so that they can say with Isaiah, 'Here am I and the children whom the Lord has given me!' (*Isa.* 8:18). And let them preach so that they can return their commission with these words: 'You gave me this people, Lord, and told me to deliver them, so that they do not go down into hell. I have done it. It is the thing my soul aimed at with all my energy and desire. By your mercy I have completed the task.'

All Christian ministers must aim at saving souls all the more seriously because the Antichrist pursues the destruction of souls by winning them to his synagogue.

The Moslem spares no labour and counts no cost to infect the young children of Christians with his impure and blasphemous superstitions. Similarly, the Pope and his servants (especially Jesuits) use every means, and devise many kinds of strategies sparing neither cost nor labour, to seduce and inveigle young and intelligent men. Their attention to policy and detail is admirable; but sadly, when (like the Pharisees) they have crossed land and sea to gain one convert, they make him like themselves, a child of hell (*Matt.* 23:15). Far from having a commission from God to do this, or his promised blessing,

God forbids them. His curse is on them for what they do. But if they work so hard to destroy souls without a divine commission, and incur God's curse for their labours, how much more energetic Christian ministers should be to win and redeem souls, since they have an extensive commission for their task and the great blessing of God promised for it.

Secondly, this teaching has application to fathers. First, it helps them to see both the high privilege of the call to the ministry as a commission and power to redeem from hell and damnation, and the honour that is due to it. In addition it shows wicked men (who abuse the persons or the function of the ministry) how unthankful and contemptible they are to repay evil for good. It is not surprising that evil never departs from the houses and families of such people.

Furthermore, this is enough to encourage any man to give himself to God in this calling. Consider for a moment what ministers are: the high commissioners of God. In affairs of state we have a power that is delegated only to certain valued men. It is called the high commission. It gives them the power to do great things. Anyone whose son is considered worthy of such a commission counts himself honoured indeed. But here is a higher commission – a commission from God to redeem souls from the power of hell and from the grip of the devil. This is a true high commission; so high that it was never granted from the court of heaven to any creature, except ministers. They are, therefore, the high commissioners of the high God. Would you not consider it an honour and a cause of immense happiness to bring your son to this position?

Finally, we are given instruction here about the responsibility of those who listen to the preaching of God's Word. It is to submit to it. For if the minister has a commission to redeem your soul, it must be by the Word and holy discipline. So your duty is to hear God's Word patiently, to submit yourself to it, to be taught and instructed, even to be checked and rebuked and to have your sins unveiled and your corruptions torn up.

If you want your court case to succeed, your lawyer must first discover what its weaknesses are. If your body is to be cured, your physician must cleanse it of sickness. So if your soul is to be redeemed, your minister must uncover its weakness and purge its corruption. Such teaching may seem harsh and painful; the discipline of the gospel may seem rough to you. Yet you must not rage and rebel against it, nor must you hate the minister, nor resort to personal criticism of him. Instead, submit yourself to the gospel, because it is the message and ministry of your salvation. If you respond otherwise you will both wrong the minister and frustrate his commission. And, unfortunately, you will harm yourself even more. For it is your salvation you will be frustrating.

THE CALLING OF THE MINISTRY

II

Introduction

So I said:
'Woe is me, for I am undone!
Because I am a man of unclean lips,
And I dwell in the midst of a people of unclean lips;
For my eyes have seen the King,
The LORD of hosts.'
Then one of the seraphim flew to me, having in his
hand a live coal which he had taken with the tongs
from the altar. And he touched my mouth with it,
and said:
'Behold, this has touched your lips;
Your iniquity is taken away,
And your sin purged.'
Also I heard the voice of the Lord, saying:
'Whom shall I send,
And who will go for Us?'
Then I said, 'Here am I! Send me.'
And He said, 'Go . . .'

                                              Isaiah 6:5–9.

The first five chapters of Isaiah contain the sermons
the prophet delivered during the reign of Uzziah, king of
Judah. The sixth chapter introduces those he preached in
the reign of Jotham and later. But before he either
preached or prophesied anything in King Jotham's or his
successors' days, the Lord gave a new confirmation to his
calling.

The old king, in whose days Isaiah was first called, was now dead; another succeeded him. With the coming of a new king God renews the calling and commission of the prophet. He does not give him another calling – one calling to the office of the ministry is sufficient – but he confirms the calling he had earlier given by repeating and ratifying it. This God did to Isaiah, not as an ordinary but as an extraordinary prophet. Ordinary ministers do not need a renewal of their calling, or new signs of confirmation. But in the case of extraordinary prophets, who came in an extraordinary manner to do extraordinary works, God in his wisdom confirms their calling again and again, and does so by very extraordinary means.

From this practice of the Lord we learn that we have good reason to doubt those men, as either fanciful or worse, who pretend to have extraordinary callings in these days, and yet can scarcely show us any good signs of ordinary, much less of extraordinary divine activity in their lives. If in the days when such things were more common God renewed and confirmed his extraordinary prophets' calling again and again, then certainly in our day we may quite rightly require many more wonderful signs of an extraordinary calling before we believe it. If God himself was so careful in those days to satisfy his church of the vocation of his prophet, surely the church in these days has greater reason to doubt such cases, and to require many extraordinary signs before acknowledging any such extraordinary calling. Men harm the church, and deserve both its censure and the sword of the magistrate, when they dare boldly to offer to, or impose on the church their own imaginations and dreams as extraordinary movements of God's Spirit.

This sixth chapter of the prophecy of Isaiah has two parts: (i) the means of Isaiah's confirmation (*Isa.* 6:1–4) and (ii) the confirmation itself (*Isa.* 6:5–13). The means of his confirmation is the heavenly vision he received of holy angels appearing and speaking to him. In the confirmation which follows there are three points:

1.   The effect of the vision on the prophet was to cause him to fear. It stunned him and cast him down (v. 5).

2.   The comfort he received which raised him up again (vv. 6–7).

3.   The renewing of his commission (vv. 8–13).

1. *The Vision of God*

Isaiah's fear and amazement are described in two ways.

1.   By two signs:
   (i)   A note of exclamation, 'Woe is me'.
   (ii)   A note of extreme dejection about himself, 'I am undone'.

2.   By its two causes:
   (i)   He was an unclean man, and dwelt among unclean people.
   (ii)   He had seen the Lord. 'So I said: "Woe is me, for I am undone!"'

The Fear of the Lord
The first point to note is the fear and sense of ecstasy into which the Lord drove his holy prophet, not in his anger against him but in his love for him; not as a punishment for his sin, but as an evidence of his further love. For the purpose of God in striking this fear into him was to enable him to be a true prophet, and a suitable messenger for himself.

   This may seem to be an unusual course for God to take in order to confirm and energise his servant in zeal and courage; to strike him with extreme fear, indeed to astonish and amaze him. Yet it is clear that this is the way the Lord takes. It teaches us that all true ministers, especially those appointed to speak the greatest words in his church, must be first of all marked by a great sense of fear, in the consciousness of the greatness of their function – even a sense of amazement and astonishment, full of admiration for God's glory and greatness. They represent him and bring his message. The more afraid they are and the more they shrink under the contemplation of God's majesty and their own weakness, the more likely it is that they are truly called of God and appointed for worthy purposes in his church. Anyone who steps into this function without fear puts himself forward, but it is doubtful whether he is called by God as the prophet Isaiah clearly was.

Nor is such fear limited to Isaiah. Whenever God called any of his servants to any great work, he first drove them into this sense of fear and amazement. That is evident in Moses (*Exod.* 3:11), Jeremiah (*Jer.* 1:6), Paul (*Acts* 9:5), and others. The reason for this is clear; man's nature is always ready to take too much upon itself. God therefore in his wisdom puts a bridle into the corrupt nature of man and stuns him, lest he presume too much and trust himself too much.

In addition, a minister must teach his people to fear and reverence the Lord. But how can he teach others when he has not tied that bond in his own conscience and has never been cast down in admiration of God's glory and majesty? In addition, the ministry is a high and excellent calling (especially the office of extraordinary prophets in the Old Testament). A minister is therefore subject to pride and to being puffed up with self-conceit. Consequently Paul warns Timothy, that a minister may not be a young scholar, 'lest being puffed up with pride he fall into the same condemnation as the devil' (*1 Tim.* 3:6), indicating that it is the special danger of ministers to have high opinions of themselves because of the high dignity of their service. To prevent this, God in his mercy has planned that all true ministers will by some means or other be humbled and emptied themselves. They will be driven to such fear and amazement at the sight of their own wickedness, that they will throw themselves down at Christ's feet, and deny themselves wholly, acknowledging that anything they are they are only in him, and rely and trust only on his grace and help.

This doctrine is relevant to all ministers, but particularly for those of us who live in the university. We live as it were in a seminary; many of us are by God's grace to be directed to the ministry, as some of us already have been. We have many occasions to be puffed up in self-conceit. We see ourselves grow in age, in degrees, in learning, in honour, in reputation and estimation. To many of us God gives an abundant supply of his gifts. But there are many temptations to allure us to pride and over-inflated opinions of our own value. So let us remember that the goal we aim at is not human or carnal. Since our purpose is to save souls, the weapons of our war must not be carnal ones (*2 Cor.* 10:4) – such as pride, vanity and conceit.

If we ever aim to be made instruments of God's glory in saving souls, then at the outset let us set before our eyes not the honour but the danger of our calling, and 'Humble [y]ourselves under the mighty hand of God, that he may exalt . . . in due time' (*1 Pet.* 5:6). Let us be content for God to employ any occasion or means to pull us down either by outward crosses or inward temptation. And let us rejoice when we are humbled so that we cry out from overwhelmed spirits, as Isaiah did: 'Woe is me, for I am undone'. Otherwise if we follow the direction of our proud natures and trust in our own ability, gifts and learning, we are using carnal weapons in a spiritual warfare. Be assured that in this case the Lord will do no great work in his church by our ministry. We may raise ourselves in worldly estimation and work out our own purposes, but we will do little for the salvation of souls. It is those who often say to themselves, 'Woe is me, for I am undone', who pronounce the most powerful blessings on other men's souls, and speak the best words of comfort to other men's consciences.

Furthermore before this vision and revelation of God's glory to him Isaiah cries out, '*Woe is me, for I am undone*'. These words express extreme fear and astonishment, they express a sense of dejection that verges almost on desperation. The prophet did not believe in the intercession of angels and saints for particular men. If he had he would not have cried out at the sight of God's majesty: 'Woe is me, for I am undone'. He would have consoled himself with these thoughts: 'I will ask Moses, Samuel or David, to pray to this glorious God for me.' Or, 'Here are holy angels, seraphim, present; they see my needy situation; I will ask them to speak to this glorious and mighty Lord for me, lest I perish in this fear.' But seeing the Lord appear in majesty, and fearing his just wrath (knowing he was guilty because of his corruption) without any hope or expectation, and without the least thought of help or assistance from any creature, Isaiah cries out, 'I am undone'.

Lastly, he exclaims, 'Woe is me, *for I am undone*'. These are the words of a soul that has been humbled and cast down. He shows that he feels himself to be in the same condition as a poor sinner is when the preaching of the law has humbled him by showing him his sins and his extreme danger because of them. We thus learn that to be called to the ministry is to be, as it were, converted and regenerated. When a man is called it is a work little less than that by which God calls a sinner from sin to repentance.

God first casts down the sinner before he gives him

grace, or any sense of his love in Christ. In the same way he first humbles and casts down the prophet in the sight of God's majesty and his own misery, before he honours him with a commission to preach his Word to his people. I note this against those men who think it an ordinary matter to enter into the ministry, as many do, simply for worldly and political purposes. Some think that if a man has learning, degrees and age he is qualified for this calling. But, alas, this is not all that is needed; there is a greater work to be accomplished. He must be humbled and cast down at the sight of the greatness of such a calling, of the majesty of the God on whose behalf he is to minister, and of his own unworthiness for such great work. He must be resolved that to call a man to the ministry is the greatest work God does in his church next to the converting of a sinner and calling him into the state of grace. In fact, it is a similar work to it, for as a sinner in his conversion so a preacher when he is called will often cry out in amazement: 'Woe is me, I am undone'. So, just as they are seriously deceived who think that holiness or sanctification can sufficiently qualify a man without learning, no less so are those who think that outward abilities are sufficient without this work which was wrought in the holy prophet.

Unclean Prophet
Isaiah's confession follows: 'Because I am a man of unclean lips'. The cause of his fear is twofold.

The first element is his own uncleanness and sinfulness, and the sinfulness of his people. His own he freely confesses: 'I am a man of unclean lips'; that is, I am a miserable and sinful man and therefore I fear and tremble to stand in God's presence; I dare not look upon the Lord because of my sins.

It may be asked: How could the prophet honestly say

this? He was a holy man, and justified in God's presence by his faith in the Messiah, and sanctified by repentance. Can a man who is justified and sanctified say he is polluted? It is certain that Isaiah was so; he therefore complains here not of any great and enormous sins which he had committed to the public scandal of the church, but of the corruption of his nature. As with all men, his is a sea of iniquity, and that always appears greater the nearer a man comes to God. It was therefore now unveiled in the prophet when he was in the presence of the Lord himself.

Secondly he complains of some actual sins in his life, probably sins of omission rather than of commission. We have no evidence that the prophet was ever guilty of any great sin, and where we are ignorant of such things we are bound by charity not to imagine them. It is more probable that he complains of some smaller faults or negligence in his ministry such as not preaching to the people on some occasion when he should have; or not preaching as willingly or cheerfully as he should; or wanting to stop preaching because the people were stubborn and disobedient, or becoming impatient in his ministry when the people were rebellious and resisted his teaching. It vexed him (as it did Jeremiah) that the Jews were such a stubborn and stiff-necked people. Or it may be that he was conscious of a lack of zeal or boldness. These or similar things were the cause of his fear. An awareness of them made him cry out that he could not stand in the sight of God.

From this we learn, first of all, what a tender conscience godly ministers should have. They must make a matter of conscience not only of great and offensive sins, but even of the lowest and least sins. A minister must endeavour in his calling not only to be free of great crimes, but as far as possible be free from the least expression of evil and the least negligence. For a small fault in other men is a great one in ministers, and what may be to a certain extent pardonable in other men is not so in them. They must therefore watch over themselves very carefully and guard all their ways. With this in view, a minister in godly wisdom must often deprive himself even of things which it may be lawful for him to use, lest his liberty be an occasion of evil to others. He must abstain from the least sins lest they be blemishes to his calling, and burdens to his conscience. Consequently a minister cannot be too careful about his words, diet, company, recreation, apparel, gestures, and his whole bearing because little sins are magnified in him. Ministers must here learn the apostle's lesson, to be 'instant in season and out of season; to preach and exhort, to comfort and rebuke, publicly and privately'; to good, to bad; when it is well taken, when it is ill taken; when they willingly receive it, and when they stubbornly resist it; when they commend him and reward him, and when they criticise him and persecute him for it. Thus he must be diligent in season and out of season, for the least negligence in his duty or the omitting of the least opportunity of doing good, will, when God visits his conscience, be a burden and grief to him, as it was here to the prophet.

Furthermore if these small sins afflicted the prophet, what is to be thought of ministers who have no conscience about foul and scandalous sins? How much will lack of self-control, money-making, inhospitality, covetousness, ignorance, idleness, absence from the flock and similar shameful behaviour oppress and burden the soul, when the smallest sins stained the conscience of this holy man? Surely when God visits them their situation will be fearful. No man's predicament will be more miserable than a careless minister's. Though now such loose and immoral ministers seem to live happily and without any fear, when God appears to their conscience they will cry out in fearful anguish, 'Woe is me, for I am undone'.

Again, if such small faults so overcame this holy prophet and burdened his conscience, then what pathetic consciences must ministers have who, despite daily negligence and carelessness in their sphere of service are not touched? These men do not have the tender conscience of Isaiah. Either he was much more sensitive than he needed to be, or else these men will prove to be in a miserable state.

Lastly, let ministers with tender consciences be comforted by the example of the prophet. Who is there who does not find imperfections and blemishes in himself, which will often make him cry out, 'Woe is me'? That should not bring discomfort but joy, that they can see their own weakness as the prophet did here. If they have cause to complain about themselves they are not alone. This was the case with every holy prophet before them. In having imperfections they are no more miserable than the prophet was. But they should strive to be as blessed in seeing and lamenting their spiritual condition as he was!

Let every minister assure himself that the more conscientious he is, even about the least sins, the more he resembles the holy prophets of old, and the more likely he is to work effectually in his ministry. For his duty is to teach his people to have a conscience not only about great sins, but about all sin. But how can he do that if he has not first of all done it himself? Thus it is that godly ministers find faults in themselves when other men cannot, and cry out against themselves for their uncleanness (as Isaiah did here), when no-one would dream of accusing them of the least crime. When other men praise God for his graces in them and praise their gifts and commend their good lives, they condemn themselves and speak against their own corruptions. Their least carelessness and omissions are like great wounds in their consciences; their smallest sins and most pardonable infirmities are sore burdens to them; for of all men in the world a godly minister is a man of tender conscience.

So far the prophet has complained generally of his uncleanness and also particularly of the uncleanness of his lips. But why does he complain of the uncleanness of his *lips*, rather than of his heart, or his hands, or any other part? Were they not unclean? Yes, all in some measure. Was he not grieved at them all? Yes indeed. But he was a prophet; his duty was to use his tongue. Since a minister is an interpreter (*Job* 33:23), speaking for the people to God in prayer, and for God to the people by preaching, he is both God's mouth and the people's mouth.

The tongue of a minister is that part of his body which is to be used as the principal instrument of God's glory, and more than any other is to set forth his honour. Now every man is to be assessed in terms of his calling, rather than by anything else. Consequently the honour or dishonour of a minister depends on the use or abuse of his tongue, and his comfort or discomfort depends on whether or not he uses it well. The prophet is here full of fear at God's presence, and withdraws into himself; his conscience rebukes him for the sins which are most relevant to his work, for faults or negligence in his ministry. That is why he condemns the uncleanness of his lips.

From this we may learn several important things.

First, the emptiness of Roman Catholic teaching which magnifies the merits of the works of holy men. This holy prophet, although he was truly justified and extraordinarily sanctified, did not dare to stand before God in this partial manifestation of his glory, despite all his zeal, courage, clear conscience, effort or suffering in his ministry. In fact he was so far from being conceited about his own worth that he cried out 'Woe is me, for I am undone'. How then can we who are no better than he (and in fact much worse) stand before God in the day of judgment, in the full revelation of his infinite justice and glory? Instead we should be as Isaiah was: the smallest uncleanness of his lips and negligence in his calling drove away any pride in his own merit when he came into the presence of God. A proper consideration of our pollutions – much deeper than his – should shatter all our conceit about our own goodness, when we appear before God. Sadly Roman Catholics, who magnify their own merits, seldom if ever give serious consideration to their own infirmities, and seldom present themselves in the presence of God's majesty. If they did, the least sight of their least pollution would deliver them from ever thinking of their own merits.

Roman Catholics also speak of works of supererogation. But clearly this holy prophet had none. They teach that a man may in this life perfectly fulfil the law; but who can do that, if not ministers? And which ministers, if not extraordinary prophets? Yet here Isaiah (the chief of them) poignantly condemns his pollutions. Doubtless, if Roman Catholics would cease this self-flattering and instead of examining their consciences by their own self-pleasing corruption, present themselves before the face and presence of God's majesty, they would be far from such self-conceit.

Furthermore the prophet laments the uncleanness of his lips as the distinctive sin of his office. Ministers are thus taught to avoid that sin above all others, and to strive to fulfil that duty more than any other. Success here is his greatest comfort, the lack of it is his greatest trial. His tongue is the instrument given him to honour

God. If he uses it well, it yields him comfort, more than any other duties. But if he fails to use it, or abuses his tongue, the uncleanness of his lips will be the heaviest burden of all. It is a great mistake to think a minister can discharge his duty without preaching, or showing hospitality, and making peace among his neighbours, and performing other works of charity and virtue. But if a minister lacks this virtue, he has none at all. If he does not preach, if he abuses his lips, or if he does not open them, he has no conscience nor can have any comfort; for this is the principal duty of a minister (though all the others are required to make him a complete minister). The lack of them may condemn him before men, but it is the uncleanness of his lips which rebukes him before God, as we see here in the case of Isaiah.

The conclusion then, for every minister, is that if he had all the virtues and good properties that commend a man in the world, but if his lips are unclean (either by not preaching, or by negligent, idle or careless preaching) this uncleanness will stain his conscience and burden him in the presence of God. Then the time will come (notwithstanding all his other good qualities) when he will cry out in a far more poignant manner than Isaiah does here: 'Woe is me, for I am undone! Because I am a man of unclean lips'.

Unclean People

Isaiah now adds, 'And I dwell in the midst of a people of unclean lips'. He not only complains of his own uncleanness, but also of those among whom he lived. He does this for the following reasons: First, to teach us that it is the minister's duty to confess not only his own sins but the sins of his people, and to lament them before God. For since he is the people's interpreter to God, he must not think it sufficient to express their petitions, to unfold their wants and plead for their relief at God's hand. He must also be conscious of the sins of his people, and publicly and privately confess them to God. The more precisely he can do this the better, both for the people's good and for his own, because it cannot but be that the sins of his people are in some sense his too. This is the special danger of the magistrate's and minister's calling, that generally the sins of their people are theirs too. I mean that they are accessories to the sins of their people, either by provoking them by their evil example, or by not reproving, or not hindering or permitting, or turning a blind eye to, or covering and concealing, or not punishing them, or not carefully enough using means to prevent them. By these and many other means the people's sins are the minister's by communication. Thus for his own sake as well as for theirs, he is to confess their sins as well as his own to God.

If a minister must confess his people's sins, it follows that he must know them, and take notice of them; otherwise he cannot confess them. This is one reason why the Holy Spirit commands a pastor 'to know his flocks' (*Prov.* 27:23). He must not only have a flock, and know which is his flock, or have a general interest in it. He must have an intimate and distinct knowledge of the state of it, the more detailed the better.

If the minister ought to know and confess his people's sins then it follows, first, that it is best for a minister to be present with his people, so that he may the better know them and their state. And certainly if it is a minister's duty to confess his people's sin to God, then wilful and careless absence as well as any absence without right and proper reasons, must be a serious and fearful sin. For how could Isaiah have confessed that his people were a people of unclean lips if he did not dwell among them? No, says the prophet, he lived 'in the midst of them'. Well may he know and confess his people's pollutions who lives in the midst of them!

Again, if the minister is to confess his people's sins, and must therefore know them, it follows also that they must confess them to him, or it will not be possible for him perfectly to know their condition. The lack of this is a great fault in our churches. We rightly condemn auricular confession as a subtle strategy and a rack to the consciences of poor Christians. But we not only permit, we actively encourage the kind of confession in which a Christian may at all times freely go to his pastor and open his heart, unburdening his conscience of the sins that disturb him, and ask for his godly assistance and holy prayers. Great blessing and comfort doubtless come to those who use this godly practice. The lack of it means that a minister cannot discern the state even of his own flock, nor intercede with God about their blemishes and confess their sins as accurately as would be good both for him and them.

Secondly, the prophet couples together his own pollution and the pollution of his people as the helping cause and the effect. For the pollution of a people helps forward the pollution of a minister, and the worse people they are, the worse they make him, even although he is in other respects an excellent man. For even the prophet, though called of God himself and justified and sanctified, and a man of extraordinary grace, yet dwelling in the midst of a people as stubborn and disobedient as the Jews was influenced by their pollutions. Ministers (even the best) are men, and this happens because of the corruption of their nature as men. The nature of this corruption is to catch any evil wherever it finds it, and to share in it.

Regeneration qualifies and moderates this corruption, but does not take it away totally in this life. Thus a minister, living among evil people, cannot but be partly stained with their pollution. This is why it often happens that a man known to be otherwise inclined in himself is found to be disposed to this or that evil by living among a people so inclined. And again, that a minister in such a place, and among such people, free from certain sins, who moves to another place, is there found more or less tainted with them because they abound among the people. And also that a minister known to be faithful, hard-working and zealous, who comes to a disobedient and stubborn, self-willed, or profane and dissolute people, has his faith weakened, his zeal and courage abated, God's graces in him dulled and much decayed. Godly ministers complain daily of this, and experience everywhere shows it to be only too true. Out of this we may learn something both for our instruction, and for our behaviour.

We learn here how wicked and wretched the corruption of our nature is, when it cannot help being infected by the pollution of those with whom we live. This is true not only of those who live with a loose rein over themselves, but even those who carefully scrutinise their steps; as we see here in this holy prophet, who was a man of more than average sanctification. There is little reason for any man to extol nature. The schoolmen and some other Roman Catholics had even less cause to give the least commendation to our natural ability. For if nature rectified by grace can hardly be kept under control, how outrageous and perverse is it when it reigns without control?

In addition we learn here what an insidious, encroaching nature sin has. Like a secret venom in the physical body, so in the body politic it is not confined to the place or party infected but creeps and spreads into every part and member of the whole. It spreads from man to man, yes, from an evil man to a good one, and from the worst man to the best, from profane men to godly ministers, and so from public persons (like magistrates and ministers) it descends visibly, and the example of their evil life is clearly scandalous. So from the people to the magistrate or minister, it creeps secretly, and ascends in an even more secret and undetected manner. Yet in its effects it is all too tangible, for it is always seen that they are infected by their people's pollutions. Sin is not only like a poison spreading from the heart to all parts, from the minister to the people; it is also like gangrene; if it begins in the foot, without speedy preventative measures it will affect the heart itself. So sin makes its presence felt from the people to the ministers. There is, therefore, serious cause for all men to stop sin in the beginning, to nip it in the bud, to give water no passage, not even a little; for allow this gangrene to begin at the feet and it will not rest until it affects the heart itself.

As far as our behaviour is concerned we learn various lessons here. First, if a minister, because of the corruption of his own nature and the creeping nature of sin is in such danger of being stained with the people's pollutions, then let all ministers desire and use every legitimate means to dwell with people who are as little polluted as possible. Otherwise let him be sure he will be polluted with them, which will both wound his own conscience (as it did the prophet), and bring disgrace to his profession. For if it is the duty of every good professor of religion, 'to keep himself unspotted from the world' (*James* 1:27), then how much more is it the minister's duty? And how deep a stain is it to the honour of his calling to be polluted with the common pollutions of the people?

It is therefore good counsel to all godly ministers seeking a place of service, not to enquire only about the stipend of a church, how well situated it is, how healthy and beneficial it will be (which are, sadly, the common and almost the only questions asked nowadays), but to be concerned principally about the character of the people, and how spiritually-minded they are, among whom they are to live. If they are godly and well disposed, or at least teachable and decent, then he should be less concerned about other problems. But if they are wicked and profane, or worse – stubborn, self-willed and unteachable – then the most comfortable circumstances will not be a compensation. If this point is given serious consideration (and how bitter it has been in the end to many who have not taken account of it) it will be clear that this is the best encouragement or discouragement, the greatest convenience or inconvenience, and the best reason either to win a man to a place or to draw him from it, however good it be in other ways. Those who neglect this duty, and are led (or rather misled) with carnal and worldly concerns, get only what they deserve when they are made to cry in the sorrow of their soul, 'Woe is me, . . . I dwell in the midst of a people of unclean lips'.

In the light of this, ministers who have small stipends but good people should not grow weary or be discouraged. They have more cause to bless God than to be grieved, for they are far better off than those who have high stipends but evil people. As for those to whom God has been so good as to give them adequate livings and a willing and well-disposed people, let them think themselves doubly blessed by God, and treble bound to honour him and to do good in his church. If such men do not excel their brethren in ministerial care and duty, their fault is above all men and they are unworthy of such great mercies.

Again, if a polluted people infect their minister, this

should act as a warning for all ministers to be wary and careful about the company in which they have private fellowship. For they may neither retire into isolation, nor stay apart from all contact with their people (which would be a cynical and bizarre, not a religious, practice). Of all men they must be careful to avoid carelessly and lightly spending their time in all kinds of company, as too many do in our church, and cause great offence. They do not care with whom they converse: all kinds of company, all places, all times, all sports and recreations, all meetings, all occasions, are one and the same to them. Sadly, it is no surprise if such men do not 'keep themselves unspotted from the world', but are an offence to their calling. Since the best men cannot live with the best people without being contaminated by them, ordinary ministers must learn to differentiate men and meetings, times and places, and not in a widespread and careless fashion involve themselves in them. Only thus can they keep their calling free from reproach and preserve themselves from pollution, which will otherwise contaminate them.

Here people should be counselled not to censure their minister too sharply if he is not as sociable with them as many expect, for no-one needs to be as wary of his company and pastimes as a minister. If people want to be strengthened and honoured by their minister, let them be careful about the activities and company they introduce him to or want him to share. The more polluted the people are among whom he lives, the more careful he must be to keep himself clean.

Lastly, people are taught not to be too sharply condemnatory of ministers whose lives are not as perfect as we would wish. If they live poorly, generally the cause is because they live among similar people. Why should they condemn them for faults which they themselves have encouraged? I do not deny that our church and state and ministry should censure such men (it would be good if they did it more frequently). But it is against all reason for the people to do so, if they themselves are the cause of it. For if this holy prophet was a man of unclean lips, because he dwelt with a people of unclean lips, it should be no surprise if ordinary ministers are contaminated by the common and widespread pollutions of their people.

People therefore should first of all see that they themselves are well ordered and godly, and then they may complain if the lives of their ministers are not. Otherwise, it is not possible, without very special grace from God, for a minister to avoid being more or less influenced by the common faults of his people. Sadly daily experience shows us that where people in a town are given to drunkenness, there the minister tends to become the same in order to have company, or at least becomes far too sociable. Where people are given to contention, there the minister has too many law-suits; where the people have Roman Catholic tendencies, there the minister is too superstitious; where the people are ignorant, there the minister is no great scholar; where the people are given to any great sin, there the minister generally is not free from the same pollution.

It is well known that the best and most careful ministers complain bitterly of the pollutions of their people. Even if they escape sharing their sins, they always find at least a dulling and decaying of God's graces in themselves if their people are difficult and disobedient. If a minister lives with such a people, his situation is a dangerous one; he deserves to be on our hearts, for he walks through nets and snares set to trap him on every side. If he escapes them (I mean, if he keeps himself unspotted among a polluted people), his self-discipline and his conscience are worthy of both admiration and imitation, and he is worthy of double honour as both a zealous minister and a holy man. But the minister whom God has blessed with a good and easily-led people who are well disposed to the Word, but who lives carelessly and scandalously among them, creates a weighty burden and a heavy debt. No rebuke is too rough, no punishment too great, no censure too sharp for him. If this holy prophet feared the presence of God because of his small heart-pollution and yet lived among so wicked and contaminated a people, then what a weight of horror shall be heaped on the soul of someone who does not care what pollution stains him while he lives among a godly and well-disposed people? Thus we have the first cause of his fear – his own, and his people's pollutions.

The Presence of God
The second cause of the prophet's fear and astonishment is that he saw the Lord who appeared in glory to him: 'For my eyes have seen the King, the Lord of Hosts.' He did not see the substance of God (for that is invisible and incomprehensible) but his glory. Nor did he see the fullness of his glory, for that cannot be endured. He was given only a glimpse of it. Nor did he even see this with his physical eyes in the ordinary way, but in a vision. To what extent physical sight was involved neither the prophet expresses nor can we easily tell. The meaning is simply that he saw in a vision such glory and majesty that he knew there was an extraordinary presence of the Lord of Hosts who is the King of glory – at whose sight and at the thought of whose presence his conscience was smitten with fear because of his own infirmities and the pollutions of his people.

We should first notice the connection between these two causes and their dependence on each other. Since they are jointly the cause of his fear, one of them is in a sense the cause of the other. He fears because of his own and his people's sins, and because he saw the Lord. But why is he afraid to see the Lord? Precisely because of his and their sins, without which he would never have been afraid; rather he would have gloried in seeing the Lord. But his conscience restrained him. Because he has failed in the duties of his calling he trembles at the least glimpse of God's glory. Here notice the ground of his reason which is this: the man who lives in sin is not able to stand in the presence of God. This is a general and certain truth. The reasons for it are:

First, the antithesis between God and the nature of sin. It is the only thing which offends him, and which provokes his wrath and just displeasure. A subject cannot but be alarmed if he realises that he has entered the king's presence with anything which the king hates or cannot bear to see. In the same way we experience deep spiritual shock when we realise that we are in God's presence with sins which he hates.

Secondly, sin makes a man a debtor to God. The law ties him first to obedience. If he sins and fails it binds him to punishment; and the more a man sins, the deeper he is in God's debt. If then in this world a man cannot bear the sight of him in whose debt he is, it is not surprising that a poor sinner trembles at the presence of the God to whom he has forfeited his soul and everything he possesses.

Thirdly, sin provokes God to wrath. Consequently a sinful man fears the presence of God as a traitor fears the face of the prince or a criminal of the judge. For these reasons a wicked man cannot endure God's presence.

Now God's presence has various degrees:

1.   God is present to our conscience, when we think of him.

2.   He is present when we name him, or hear him named or mentioned by others.

3.   God is nearer to us in the presence of his ordinances such as his Word and sacraments and public worship in the congregation.

4.   There is a particular sense of the presence of God at the last judgment, when all men shall stand before him in his immediate presence to receive his judgment on them.

In each of these senses the presence of God is hated by the wicked.

As to the first, a wicked man will not willingly think of God, and if sometimes a thought of God flashes like lightning into his mind, he immediately quenches it as unwelcome and burdensome. Therefore David says: 'The wicked in his proud countenance does not seek God; God is in none of his thoughts' (*Psa.* 10:4). They think so little about God himself that they will not willingly think of anything that might bring God into their thoughts – such as God's great works of wonderful judgment, of which the same prophet says in the same psalm: 'Your judgments are far above, out of his sight' (*Psa.* 10:5). It is as if he had said that he strains to put them as far as possible from the eye of his mind, so that he may have no reason to think about them, nor of God because of them. That this is true of his thoughts, I have tried to prove by God's own testimonies, because thoughts cannot be discerned by man.

As for the second, that is, for his words, this is obvious for all to see. You will never see a wicked man willingly and gladly have God in his mouth (unless it is to abuse his name, by swearing or blasphemy), nor willingly hear anyone else talk about God or of his greatness and his justice. Such talk is tedious and burdensome to him; and if he cannot divert it with other topics of conversation he sits as silent as a fish, and inwardly either frets with anger or is tormented with fear. All this was true of Felix the governor who trembled while Paul 'reasoned about righteousness, self-control, and the judgment to come' (*Acts* 24:25).

As to the third, we daily see wicked men who cannot stand God's presence in the church. Nothing is more irritating to them than many sermons, frequent praying and receiving the Lord's Supper. But further than that, as the psalmist says, 'they do not call on the Lord' (*Psa.* 14:4). The last judgment they fear and abhor most of all, and hope in their hearts it may never happen. Paul mentions that it is the mark of a true believer and a holy man to love and look for the appearing of Jesus Christ (*2 Tim.* 4:8). It follows that it is a sign of a wicked man to fear the last judgment, and to wish it might never be. And when they see they cannot escape it, what then can they do? They will 'say to the mountains and rocks, "Fall on us and hide us"' (*Rev.* 6:16). From what? 'From the presence of God'. That is the measure of how fearful and hateful God's presence is to a sinful man.

There is one further way in which God shows his presence: by an extraordinary and immediate revelation of his glory. This was normal in the Old Testament (as here), but it is not now to be expected. But how terrible that is to the sinful nature of man is made clear here. If a holy man such as the prophet, whose conscience accused him of a few small sins only, thus cries out, amazed and terrified by the revelation of God's glory, how much more terrifying will it be to those whose consciences are burdened with great and grievous sins, without repentance? Thus we see why it is true that a man in his sin cannot cheerfully come before or boldly stand in God's presence.

Practical Implications

1.   First of all let us see the extreme presumption of
ministers who rashly enter the ministry. They tread on
the holy ground of God with unclean feet, and handle
the holy things of God with unwashed hands. For what is
it to enter into the ministry but to enter into the chamber
of the presence of the great King? Should not a man
look about him before he comes there? God rebuked
Moses for stepping too hastily towards the bush where
his presence was, and said, 'Do not draw near this place
. . . for the place where you stand is holy ground'
(*Exod.* 3:5). How, then, will he rebuke and check the
consciences of carnal men who carelessly and carnally
rush into the pulpit, and to God's table, where God is
present in an even greater manner than he was in the
bush? If men who enter into this calling without fear and
reverence are to be blamed, how much more faulty are
those ministers who venture to preach or minister the
holy sacraments without holy and private preparation
and sanctification, and rush into them as though they
were common, secular actions? God is present there in
a holy and glorious way. These men will say that the
prophet's conscience was too sensitive. But God will
appear as fearful and awesome at the last to men who do
not care how they appear in his holy presence.

This explains the reason for the practice in all
Christian churches of prayer before and after the sermon.
This is not for decorum merely, to grace the action, but
to sanctify and to humble ourselves. We are coming
before God's presence! We do not think reverently
enough of God and his presence if our practice is to the
contrary.

Furthermore, we learn here the serious situation of
those ministers who are so presumptuous as to exercise
that holy function but who remain in their sins without

repentance. What do these men do? They approach the burning bush with their shoes on their feet, entering into God's presence in their sins. What will be the end result of this? The burning fire shall consume them. The least sin and smallest negligence filled the holy prophet with fear when he went into God's presence. Yet these men dare to come into the sanctuary of God, they dare to take God's Word in their mouths, and yet hate to be reformed. They cast the glorious Word of God behind their backs (*Psa.* 50:16–17), although they preach to others with their mouths. These men may express surprise at this holy prophet's sensitivity but the whole world is amazed at their profaneness. A little pollution of his lips made Isaiah afraid to come into God's presence; but these men dare to come with eyes, ears, lips, feet, hands, heart, all polluted. Their eyes polluted with careless looking at vanities; their ears with hearing; and their lips with careless and sinful talk; their feet with running into wicked company; their hands with practising and their hearts with devising and consenting to all manner of wickedness.

This is the reason why the labours of such men are so unprofitable: they dare to come into God's presence in their sins.

In many parts of our land there is by God's blessing much teaching, yet there is little reformation in the lives of most; sadly, by contrast some fall into atheism, some into Roman Catholicism, some into foul sins which ought not to be mentioned among Christians.

What is the cause? It cannot lie in the gospel; nor in our doctrine, nor in the teaching of it.

One principal cause is that many ministers come into God's presence unsanctified, and in their sins, little concerned about how loosely they live before their people. Therefore God in his justice, although he does not instantly smite them with visible vengeance for their presumption, smites the people with spiritual blindness, so that they are not concerned about doctrine. They look only at their ministers' lives and follow the profaneness of their behaviour rather than the holiness of their words. God desires to be sanctified in his ministers. Because they do not sanctify but rather dishonour him by coming into his presence in their sins, he cannot tolerate them or give any blessing to their labours.

If ministers are to see any fruit from their ministry, they must first sanctify themselves and cleanse their hearts by repentance before they presume to stand up to rebuke sin in others. Let them not think that their golden words will do as much good as their dead lives will do harm. They may possibly confirm men who are already converted, but it is highly unlikely that they will convert any soul from Roman Catholicism or profaneness. It is a vain hope for men to imagine that there is any force in eloquence or human learning to overthrow the sins of others which rule and reign in themselves. Our church, and all reformed churches, must make good use of this doctrine.

It is the glory of a church to have its doctrine powerful and effectual for the winning of souls. Churches should, therefore, make sure that their ministers are godly men as well as good scholars, and that their lives are inoffensive as well as their doctrine sound. Otherwise they will find through painful experience that they pull down as much with one hand as they build up with the other.

But most of all this doctrine concerns ministers themselves. They must know that their case is the most fearful of all if they come into God's presence in their profane condition. As no man is more honourable than a learned and holy minister, so none is more contemptible in this world and none more miserable for that to come, than one who by his loose and immoral life brings disgrace on his teaching. He must learn that, for his presumption in rushing into God's presence in his sins, he will, in this world, be cast out as unsavoury and 'trampled underfoot by men' (*Matt.* 5:13) with contemptuous feet. And in the world to come he will above all men cry out in the most extreme torment of conscience, 'Woe is me that my eyes must see the King, the Lord of Hosts.' Because he would not in this world come into God's presence in sanctification and holiness, he shall in fear and horror be hauled into the presence of God's glory at the last day to receive the just sentence of his condemnation.

Lastly, all conscientious and godly ministers may receive comfort here not to be discouraged or driven from God's presence because of their sinfulness or weakness. We see here that this was the prophet's case. Let them still approach in fear and reverence. Far from being driven from their duty, because as sinful men they dare not come into God's presence as sinners without much fear, let them be assured that the more they tremble at God's presence here the less they will need to fear it at the last day. Profane and ungodly men who did not fear in this world to stand in God's presence in their sins will cry to the mountains, 'Fall on us', and to the hills, 'Cover us, and hide us from the presence of God.' Then ministers who approached God's presence in this world in fear and trembling and always in repentance, will look up, lift up their heads, and say to the holy angels and all the powers of heaven: 'Help us, and hurry us into the glorious presence of our God and Saviour'. And thus we see the manifold use of this doctrine to our church and ministry.

2.   Secondly, conscious of his corruptions, the prophet cries out in fear at the least revelation of God's glory.

The empty falsehood of the Church of Rome is here unmasked. In its legends of the saints nothing is more common than the appearances of departed saints, of glorious angels and of the virgin Mary (with such familiarity that she sometimes sang with them in their cells, kissed some of them, and let them suck her breasts). Indeed appearances of God himself are claimed and especially of our Saviour Christ Jesus, who they say appeared (countless times it seems) to one man, St Francis. He is supposed to have appeared as he was crucified, with his wounds, and to have imprinted his wounds on Francis' body. They then claim that he bore them all his life, and that they bled whenever he allowed them – which he always did on Good Friday – so that he might be like Christ.

More directly to the point: If apparitions from heaven are such everyday events in the Roman Catholic Church how can it be that the greatest and holiest men in the Old Testament were so amazed when an angel appeared? Some ran away and hid themselves, some covered their faces, others fell flat on the ground. Isaiah here cried out, 'Woe is me, for I am undone! For my eyes have seen the King, the Lord of Hosts.'

Contrast this with the Church of Rome. A saint or monk is a nobody unless he has had some apparition, either of the virgin Mary or one of the apostles, or an angel, or Christ Jesus himself appearing and talking with him. But Peter, James and John, those three great pillars (*Gal.* 2:9), were almost beside themselves when they were given a glimpse of a little part of the glory of Christ in his transfiguration (*Matt.* 17:6; *Luke* 9:33)!

Either these men have no sin and can dare to behold God's glory as casually as they do (which is impossible), or rather (which is the truth of the matter) these are illusory day-dreams, forgeries of their own creation in order to deceive the world and to boost themselves in the eyes of the general public.

In the first place it is simply false to claim that such 'showings' are as common as they make out. If they are, why were they even more infrequent in the New Testament than in the Old? For where the Scripture has one, their legends have twenty; whereas only one person in the New Testament, the apostle Paul, was once 'caught up to the third heaven' (*2 Cor.* 12:2), they can list twenty who were caught up there. That is just as false as the idea that any man clothed with flesh can endure the extraordinary appearance of God's glory without total amazement. That is clear here in Isaiah. He was as holy a man as the holiest monk.

I mention this so that young ministers may be encouraged to probe under the surface of these legends and discover the false tricks and manipulativeness of the religion that accompanies them. It would not need to resort to such evil tricks if it were of God.

3. Thirdly, God's people may here learn the following lessons:

(i) In view of the fact that God's presence is so glorious and fearful to our nature, we learn how mercifully God has dealt with us, teaching us not by himself, or by his angels from heaven, (which we could never endure) but by men who are like ourselves. How self-assured and foolish people are who want to be taught immediately from heaven instead of through men full of needs themselves. When the people received the law from God's own mouth they ran away and cried out, 'Now therefore, why should we die? If we hear the voice of the Lord our God anymore, then we shall die. For who is there of all flesh who has heard the voice of the living God and lived?' They said to Moses, 'You go near, and hear all that the Lord our God may say, and tell us all that the Lord our God says to you, and we will hear and do it.' The next verse tell us that the Lord said, 'I have heard the words of this people which they have spoken to you. They are right in all that they have spoken' (*Deut.* 5:25–28). And so, from that day on, God ordinarily taught his church by men like themselves. That pattern began not in judgment but in mercy to them. It is therefore the duty of all of us to acknowledge this mercy of God in thankfulness, and to remember when we see weaknesses in ministers that they are only men. If they did not have the ministry through men, it would be unbearable for them. For the least measure of God's own presence cannot be endured by any man.

(ii)   Since God's presence is so glorious in itself and awe-inspiring to our nature we are taught to prepare ourselves by prayer, humiliation and by the confession of our sins and unworthiness before we come to God's Word or sacraments. For we come then into God's presence. We are not to come trusting in ourselves, nor may we come with our ordinary sins unrepented of, lest God strike our consciences with a sense of his fearful displeasure and make us cry out with greater reason than the prophet did here.

(iii)   Lastly, we learn here the different natures and properties of sin and holiness. Sin, the least sin, even the sinfulness of our nature, makes us afraid of God's presence. That unrepented sin does so is obvious in Adam. In his integrity he spoke with God in an intimate way. But no sooner had he sinned than he ran from God and hid himself. That even the least unrepented sins have the same effect is seen in Isaiah too. Although he was a holy man, his conscience was aware of small omissions and negligence in his ministry. He cried out that he was undone, because he had seen the Lord of hosts.

On the other hand, the state of perfect holiness and the absence of all sin makes a man bold in God's presence, and wanting – rather than afraid – to behold the glory of God, which will be fully revealed at the last day. For when the wicked shall desire to be covered with the hills, and ground to dust by the mountains (*Rev.* 6:16) rather than to appear before the face of God, then shall the godly, whose holiness shall then be perfect, 'look up and lift up their heads, because their redemption draws near' (*Luke* 21:28). And Job testifies that he knows his Redeemer lives, and that he shall stand before him, and look upon him with his eyes (*Job* 19:25–27). Thus, just as guilt drives a man from the king's presence but innocence makes him bold before him, so sinfulness makes a man avoid God's presence but holiness makes him draw near to God, and to rejoice in his presence.

2. *Divine Consolation*

We have seen the fear and amazement Isaiah experienced in God's presence. Now we must consider the way in which he was comforted: 'Then one of the seraphim flew to me, having in his hand a live coal which he had taken with the tongs from the altar. And he touched my mouth with it, and said: "Behold, this has touched your lips; Your iniquity is taken away, And your sin purged."'

There are two points in the text:

1.   The foundation and substance of his consolation: the forgiveness of his sin.

2.   The various circumstances of that consolation:
   (i) The time: 'Then'.
   (ii) The minister by whom it was done: an angel, 'one of the seraphim'.
   (iii) The manner in which he did it – speedily: 'he flew'.
   (iv) The instrument or outward sign: 'a live coal . . . from the altar'.
   (v) The outward application of it: he 'touched [his] lips'.

Since the matter of the consolation is last in order, we will look first at the circumstances.

The Time

The first circumstance is the specific time when the prophet was comforted and delivered from his fear. *Then*, says the text; that is, after his fear and amazement, not before. God has always thus dealt with his saints. He gives none of the graces of salvation until he has, by some means or other, brought us to a true humiliation in ourselves and to sorrow for our sins. Humiliation is the preparation for grace. When by the sight and sense of our sins and our misery because of sin, God has driven us out of ourselves so that we find nothing in ourselves but reasons for fear and horror; then he pours the oil of grace and of sweet comfort into our hearts, and refreshes our weary souls with the dew of his mercy. This point needs no further proof. If we look into the Scriptures we shall find God never called people into the state of grace or to any notable work or function in his church without first humbling them. Then he brought them out of all self-conceit and wrought in them and by them his wonderful works.

The practical value of this doctrine is, first of all, to teach all men to esteem aright the afflictions that God lays upon them in this world. Ordinarily we are impatient with them and bear grudges against them. But the Christian should consider how God has always dealt with his children. He will then have good reason not to respond like that. Does God bring some great affliction on you? It may be he has some mighty work of grace to do in you, or some great work of mercy to be wrought by you in his church, and is preparing you for it. Learn to say with the holy prophet, 'I was mute, I did not open my mouth, Because it was You who did it' (*Psa.* 39:9). What God may intend you cannot tell; therefore, in silence and patience, possess your soul.

This is a comfort to all those who are distressed because

of their sins and sense themselves to be under God's wrath. Their condition is not miserable, however. In fact it is much less desperate, for they are on the highway to grace and favour. God justifies only those who repent; he exalts only those who are humbled; he comforts none but the distressed; he has mercy only on those who both know and feel they lack it, and who also know that there is nowhere else to receive it except at his hands. Happy therefore is the person who feels the weight and burden of sin. To him Christ will bring ease and comfort. God's ministers are thus to encourage distressed consciences and to assure them that if, like the prophet, they are so deeply aware of their sins and of God's justice that they cry, 'Woe is me, for I am undone!', just 'then' they are most capable of comfort, and best prepared to receive it. That was what happened to the holy prophet.

Thirdly, we learn here the way to attain to any of the excellent graces of God, either for our own salvation or for the good of the church. We must develop a conscious sense of the lack of them in ourselves. For God does not normally bestow gifts on any except those who in humility and lowliness confess to him and acknowledge in themselves the need of them. We learn this from the example of the blessed virgin Mary: 'He has filled the hungry with good things, And the rich He has sent away empty' (*Luke* 1:53). Similarly the psalmist says: 'For He satisfies the longing soul, And fills the hungry soul with goodness' (*Psa.* 107:9). So then if you are rich in self-conceit God has nothing for you; but if you are hungry, he is ready to fill you with good things. Do you acknowledge that your soul is empty? Then there are treasures of goodness to feed and fill you. Are you cast down like Isaiah and is your soul empty of hope and fraught with fear? Then God and his angels are ready to raise you up and to fill you with consolation.

So much for the time of his consolation. Now we must consider the minister through whom it came to him.

The Agent

The second circumstance of his consolation is the minister by whom it came: an angel, one of those known as seraphim. From this we learn four things.

First, that there are different degrees and several orders of angels. We do not know exactly what distinguishes them from each other. Nor do we think it is correct to think that there are nine orders, or to describe them in detail, as the Church of Rome does, making up its own ideas (which it calls traditions) and making them of equal authority with the Scriptures.

Secondly, the holy angels are the glorious guard of God. They continually stand around the throne of his glory, and attend his holy will, both in heaven and on earth.

Thirdly, they are also, by the merciful appointment of God, the guard of God's children, and ministering spirits sent out, as it were, with a commission to see to the good of the elect. All these points are plain in the Scriptures, but less relevant to our interest here, which is the ministry, so I pass them over.

Fourthly, it is apparent that the angels are sent out to help and serve the elect, especially God's ministers. This is plain here, where the fearful prophet finds a holy angel is ready to give him comfort. The same is true of all the prophets. Even today, their protection and strengthening ministry is no less a reality to the godly ministers of the New Testament, even if it comes to us without the same signs or visible manner as in the Old. For if they are ministering spirits, sent out for the good of those who shall be saved, how much more for the good of those who shall be both saved themselves and save others too.

This is a doctrine of great comfort and value to all ministers. It brings them contentment in their calling. No calling carries more crosses, but none brings more comfort. Even if none is more disgraced by evil men, none is more honoured by the holy angels. Even although in this world they are, more than anyone else, servants to all men, yet no others experience the ministry of angels as much as they do. They do not help us to perform the outward actions of our ministry either with us, or for us (as some Roman Catholic doctors teach, so that in the mass, 'Amen' is not said to one of the collects because it is believed the angels say 'Amen' to it). Nevertheless they are present always, at all holy exercises and lawful activities, but especially at the public worship of God led by ministers. In addition, they are witnesses of these occasions and of the labours, diligence and faithfulness of good ministers. They also often minister bodily strength and assistance and many comforts to them in their troublesome travels, when they do not know by what natural means they experience them.

This doctrine gives ministers contentment in the face of the contempt and courage in the face of the danger associated with their calling. What if you have influential men of this world against you, when you have angels for you? What if you fight against principalities and powers, when you have cherubim and seraphim on your side? Godly ministers have many enemies, but if by the eye of faith they can see clearly those who are with them, as with the eye of reason they see those who are against them, they will confess with Elisha, 'Those who are with us are more than those who are with them' (*2 Kings* 6:16).

Stories from every age affirm this as does our own experience. It is amazing to see how many dangers ministers who live in ungodly places or places dominated by

Roman Catholicism have escaped, and the plots they have avoided, which their enemies (or rather the enemies of their doctrine) have schemed against their lives. Their deliverance and many other comforts in their ministries surely come from God's protection through the ministry of angels.

Before we leave this point, two relevant questions may be asked.

1. If we ask how it is that angels perform more service to good ministers than to other men, it is partly to do with God, partly to do with the angels. First, God has a principal care of them above other men, because they do his work in a more concentrated way than do other callings. Their work is immediately related to the good of men's souls. Other callings are concerned with the body first, and then with the soul. Therefore, whereas 'he has given his angels charge over all his elect, to keep them in all their ways' (*Psa.* 91:11), they have a special charge over all godly and faithful ministers since their ways are God's in a special sense.

Again, since angels willingly perform their service to the church as a whole or to any part of it, they are especially willing to be employed for the good of godly ministers. There are two reasons for this:

First, because they are their fellow-labourers. Both angels and good ministers are called God's ambassadors. They are God's own servants or officers in a more particular manner than any other calling; since their service is so similar, they share their titles in common, angels being called ministers and ministers angels, as though they were one and the same.

Secondly, the minister's duty is to convert and save souls, and this is the very work in which (next to glorifying God, and doing his will) the angels take most delight. If they are 'sent forth to minister for those who will inherit salvation' (*Heb.* 1:14), how much more willingly must they go for the good of those through whose ministry this salvation comes? And if 'there is joy in the presence of the angels of God over one sinner who repents' (*Luke* 15:10), surely they greatly love and desire to do good to those by whom sinners are converted? In these respects angels and ministers have the same name and are both employed in the same great work, namely doing good to the elect.

This is why the angel calls himself John's fellow in the Book of Revelation (19:10; 22:9). If they are fellows, fellow-servants and fellow-labourers in a special way, it is no surprise that the angels will willingly perform any service that will help or comfort godly ministers.

2. If anyone asks: If this is the case, what duties are ministers to perform to angels in return for their devoted service and special care for them above other men? A Roman Catholic writer might answer: ministers must worship them, keep their fasts and holy days, say their services, and pray to them as to their keepers and mediators. But can the king's messenger or officer not be honoured without being placed on the king's throne? Will nothing satisfy him except the crown and sceptre? Can angels not be honoured without being made gods, or saviours or mediators? I answer: we dare not go so far lest we remember the servant so much that we forget the master. Instead, since angels render such valuable service to God's ministers, this should first of all teach all men to honour the ministry in an appropriate way. For it pleases the angels when we honour good ministers whom they regard as their fellows.

Furthermore, this should teach all ministers not to content themselves with a name or title but to strive to be good and faithful. In this way they are fellows of the angels. It is a disgrace to the angels when those who are their associates are unfaithful. This should further teach us to adorn our calling by our holy lives, for as sin grieves the angels and drives them away, grace and holiness make them delight in the fellowship of men.

It may also encourage all of us to be diligent in the holy calling in which we are sure to have God's angels attending us, assisting us, protecting us and being witnesses of our faithfulness. Who would not work cheerfully at a task in which he has the angels to be a kind of fellow-worker with him? To fulfil these duties is to honour good angels. The angels will believe themselves sufficiently honoured by any minister who conscientiously performs them.

If, beside this honour, ministers want God's angels to rejoice and desire to bring joy to them, they must teach themselves to value above all things the conversion of souls rather than their own praise, or income, or pleasing men. Let them press on in their teaching and in all their activities so that the angels may see it and be witnesses of it. For if they rejoice at the conversion of a sinner (as Christ says they do), then those who most seriously aim at the conversion of sinners make them rejoice most frequently.

Thus we see both the service of angels to God's ministers and the duties they owe in turn to them. Careful consideration of this point would bring the world to a better estimation of the ministry, and would persuade fathers to dedicate their sons to it and also stir up young students to consecrate themselves to it and direct their studies to that end. No one in any other calling enjoys the special presence and assistance of God's angels as much as godly ministers do. And even if this does not lead to a deeper appreciation of the ministry, it brings comfort and contentment to all faithful ministers in their demanding calling.

The Manner

Notice how the angel performed his service to the prophet; not unwillingly or lethargically, but speedily: 'he flew'. This is not to be understood as though angels have wings; they do not have physical bodies, but are made of such spiritual substance that they act with a nimbleness and agility that is beyond the grasp of our outward senses. This statement is, then, adapted to our capacities to show how readily and speedily the angel ministered comfort to the prophet. Nothing moves as quickly as a creature that flies; and so we speak about someone who 'flies about his business'. In a similar way the Holy Spirit expresses the willingness and speed of the angel to comfort this prophet and to do the will of God.

From this we learn several important lessons:

First, what outstanding servants of God the holy angels are! They readily, willingly and speedily execute the will of their Lord. This teaches all God's servants to do the same and to imitate them in their obedience. All the more so since we pray daily, 'Your will be done on earth as it is in heaven' (*Matt.* 6:10) – on earth by us as it is in heaven by the holy angels. They do it cheerfully and without lingering; so should we. Ministers in their places, and every individual in his sphere, should apply this personally and be motivated to a cheerful alacrity in every duty. Thus they resemble the blessed angels and their actions are consistent with their prayer. On the other hand, anyone who does his duty unwillingly and unreadily is like the devil. He does God's will, but he does it against his own will. To such obedience there belongs no reward. But since 'God loves a cheerful giver' (*2 Cor.* 9:7), doubtless he also loves a cheerful worker.

Secondly we see here the love that angels have for God's children, especially for godly ministers, and how willing they are to be employed for their good. Willing-ness and readiness to do good to anyone comes from love; but yet, alas, even the best of men and all ministers, even the finest of them, are far inferior to the angels.

Ministers must learn from this never to look down on their people, but carefully to fulfil their duties of ruling and teaching. It is the essence of love to make us willingly serve those we love, no matter what their position in society is. If princes love their subjects, they will not spare any care, cost or effort – in fact they will rejoice – to do them good. They will strive to be like the angels, who are far greater than men as they in turn are greater than their subjects.

When ministers love their people they forget any personal dignity on which they might stand, and make themselves 'servants to all, that they may win some' (*1 Cor.* 9:19). And since angels fly so fast to give help and comfort to good ministers, this further teaches us to strive to be good ministers. Then we can be sure of the love of the angels and then they will serve us all most willingly. Again, let this teach us to fly as fast to fulfil our duties to God's church as the angels fly to serve us as ministers. Then God's angels will believe that their diligent and painstaking service is well worthwhile!

Finally this willing diligence of the angels, proceeding as it does from love, must challenge all Christians to perform their duties of godliness to God and of love to his church readily and cheerfully, just as God's angels do. We tend to be more concerned to be like the angels in glory in the world to come than to be like the angels in glory in this world. The wise man says, 'Do you see a man who excels in his work? He will stand before kings; he will not stand before unknown men' (*Prov.* 22:29). And surely, whoever is willing and diligent in the duties of the Christian life will stand before the King of kings in heaven. But we must say no more about the angels' service and diligence.

The Instrument

The angel used 'a coal from the altar'. A burning coal was a strange instrument for the angel to employ for such a great task as comforting the prophet. Here human reason should hide itself and worldly wisdom be confounded before the wonderful works of the Lord. God could have healed the prophet's infirmities, comforted him in his fear and given him courage in his calling without using any means. But God is pleased to use means. But what? Weak means; indeed means that seem to contradict their function. A coal of fire must touch his lips. Something we would expect would have destroyed his powers of speech, instead, by God's appointment and the power of his words, makes him speak better. From this we can learn many valuable lessons.

First, notice how God magnifies means. He can work without them, as he did in the creation, giving light to the world days before there was sun (*Gen.* 1). But since the days when the order of nature was established he generally uses means, not only in his ordinary but even in his miraculous actions. While he does not always use ordinary and direct means he does generally use means, even although they may seem contrary to his real purpose, as in the case here. The same is true in almost all the miracles in the Old and New Testament.

This serves as a recommendation to all men to use whatever good means God's providence has ordained for any duties, or for effecting anything that we are responsible to do. We are not to depend upon immediate helps from heaven, as many credulous and unrealistic men do, who are consequently often justly forsaken by God and left destitute of help, and thus exposed to shame and reproach.

Secondly, notice the mighty power of God's ordinance: it appears in weakness. The same is true with all his great works. In the creation, he brought light out of darkness; in our redemption, he brought life out of death; in our conversion, he works upon us by his Word, and by it he draws us to himself, although in all reason it would drive us from him. By it he confounds the wisdom of the world, which is naked folly to that worldly wisdom.

So here he cleanses the prophet by a coal of fire, although we would expect it would violate him. He seasons his mouth with it, although it should have burned him. God's ordinances are great, admirable and powerful, although they seem so contradictory, or so weak in themselves, or in their means.

This should teach us not to despise the sacraments, although the outward elements of bread, wine and water are weak and common and completely lifeless in themselves. Nor should we despise the ministry of the Word, although it is exercised by a weak man, as mortal and sinful as others. Since God can season the prophet's mouth and cleanse his heart by a coal of fire, it should not surprise us that he works on the consciences of men through his Word and sacraments. Again, when we see grace and holiness brought into men's hearts by the Word and sacraments let us learn not to attribute this to the dignity of either the minister or of the elements, but to the supreme power of the mighty God who could purge the prophet by a coal from the altar.

It is not altogether without relevance to note that God here sanctifies the prophet by touching his lips with a fiery coal, for this suggests that an adequate and able teacher must have a fiery tongue. For the same reason the Holy Spirit came down upon the apostles in fiery tongues (*Acts* 2:3). It may be that the one is a type of the other. Certainly they both teach us that all true and able ministers must pray and strive to have a tongue full of power and force, just like fire, to eat up the sin and corruption of the world. It is a worthy gift of God to be able to speak mildly and moderately so that our speech falls like dew upon the grass; but it is the fiery tongue that beats down sin and works sound grace in the heart. It may be that some stand in need of such a fiery tongue.

This shows that ministers who sit still while they see great and grievous stains on the church and corruption in the state, and are content never to reprove them, have never had their lips touched with a coal from God's altar. Their souls have never experienced a coal from God's altar; their consciences have never been touched nor their souls seasoned with the sanctifying grace of God's Spirit. They live as though ministers were persuaders only, and not reprovers. But when this is weighed in the balances of a good conscience it will become clear that it is not the pleasing tongue but the fiery tongue that is the principal grace of a good minister.

But to go further, where did this coal come from? It was 'taken from the altar'. It was taken by the angel from the altar of God, where there was a fire which never went out. This was the fire that came from heaven, sent by God at the dedication of the temple by Solomon. Kindled by God, it never went out. No one could kindle such fire; everything else was regarded as strange fire, as Nadab and Abihu found to their terrible cost when they tried to make their offering with it (*Lev.* 10:1-2).

The prophet had to be cleansed with the fire which came from heaven, teaching us, as we have seen, that a minister must have his fiery tongue from the Holy Spirit, just as the apostles were said to be baptised with 'the Holy Ghost and with fire' (*Acts* 1:5; *Matt.* 3:11). A fiery tongue is the special ornament of a minister; but the fire must come from heaven so that his zeal is a godly and heavenly zeal. Someone who has a censorious, a lying, a slanderous, a malicious, or a contentious tongue, has a fiery tongue indeed. But it is kindled by the fire of hell, as James says: 'The tongue is a fire, a world of iniquity. The tongue is so set among our members that it defiles the whole body, and sets on fire the course of nature; and it is set on fire by hell' (*James* 3:6).

This spiteful and malicious tongue is a fiery tongue, but its fire is taken from hell, not from God's altar. God will never allow any great work to be done in his church by anyone who stands up to preach with such a tongue, even if his tongue is fiery and his speech powerful.

Just as ministers must abhor a tongue that flatters and seeks to please men, and instead have a fiery tongue; so on the other hand, this fire must come from God's altar alone. The fire of their zeal must be kindled by God's Spirit and not by a spirit of discord and dissension. Ambitious spirits, turbulent and proud spirits, novel ideas, private quarrels – none of these have any place in the pulpit. They may make a man fiery tongued, but not with fire taken from God's altar, as the prophet's was. Such a fiery tongue never came from heaven, as the apostles' did.

The Application of the Remedy
In the words 'and touched my mouth' we find the fifth and last circumstance surrounding Isaiah's experience: the application of the remedy. The coal which is the medicine is applied by the angel to Isaiah's lips, that is to the part of him which was polluted. Since he had lamented the pollution of his lips, it is to his lips that the medicine is applied. Here the angel, who in this case is a divinely appointed minister, teaches all God's ministers

an important point of wisdom and heavenly divinity: to apply their doctrine to their hearers in a way that is appropriate to their situation, their time, or their individual experience.

Some ministers come to the ignorant and proud and try to teach them the gospel although they never knew the law. Although the fiery coal is used the lips are not touched. Good doctrine is taught but it is not well applied; for the law should first be bound on their consciences. Others emphasise the law when their hearers are already sufficiently humbled and need instead to be raised up by the comfort of the gospel. Others expose the nakedness of royalty and reprove the faults of rulers and government officials when they are preaching to ordinary people whose real need is for basic Christian teaching. Others again bring their novel or controversial ideas to ordinary congregations when these things are more appropriate for the academic world. Still others are taken up with ceremonies, and the substance of the gospel is in danger of being lost. All these have the coal of fire, but they fail to apply it to polluted lips. All ministers should learn this from the wisdom of the angel, to apply the medicine of their doctrine to the time, people and place which are actually infected. Then they will be sure that their efforts are not in vain.

The text continues: 'Your iniquity is taken away, And your sin purged.' Here is the ground and substance of his consolation; the forgiveness of his sins. Note first how it and the instrument are joined together. 'Behold,' says the angel, 'this coal has touched your lips, and your iniquity shall be taken away, and your sin purged' – as though he had been cleansed by the coal. In this way God magnifies the means which he himself ordains, attributing even the true remission of sins and salvation to a right and holy employment of them, although it does not come from them, but from his own mercy and through the power of his ordinance. It should not surprise us then if God sanctifies a child by the ministry of water in baptism, and feeds our souls in the Lord's Supper by feeding our bodies with bread and wine. Nor should it surprise us if the neglect of either of them leads to the condemnation of those who despise them, since they are God's instruments ordained by him to convey his grace to us. Yet for all this, we must realise that remission or salvation is no more tied to these elements or the actions than the prophet's forgiveness is here tied to the coal of fire.

But the main point is that, for the prophet's consolation, the angel tells him his iniquities will be taken away and his sins purged. It is as if he had said: Your sins were the cause of your fear, therefore that your fear may be taken away your sins shall be forgiven.

Here we learn that just as fear comes through sin so all true comfort comes from the forgiveness of sins. This alone pacifies the conscience and satisfies the soul. We see this in David. He had sinned against the Lord in his two great sins, provoked God's wrath and wounded his own conscience. If the prophet had told him he was being made king over ten more kingdoms, it would not have given him so much joy as when he told him when he had repented: 'The Lord also has put away your sin; you shall not die' (2 Sam. 12:13).

In the same way when Isaiah was terrified by God's presence because of some sins and carelessness in fulfilling his calling, it would have been no comfort to his poor soul to have been told: 'You shall have a more eloquent tongue, and a more powerful speech; you shall have better access to the court and a better hearing from the king.' Such encouragement would have been no better than disguised poison to him. But the happy response that refreshed his weary soul more than all the world was this: 'Behold, your iniquity is taken away, and your sin purged.'

Faithful ministers must learn from this the proper way of comforting someone with a troubled and distressed conscience: first to show him a sight of his particular sins; then to summon him into God's presence and there arraign him for those sins until the sight of their foulness and the glory of God's justice has sufficiently humbled him. Then a minister should seek to persuade his conscience on reliable grounds of the pardon of those sins by Christ Jesus. This is the way that God has designed, used and devised. It is a sure way and it cannot fail.

There are some who assume that all mental distress is nothing but depression, and consequently think nothing else is needed except medicine and physical comfort. But anyone who considers the condition Isaiah was in here, or David was in when he wrote of his experiences in Psalms 6:2-3, 6-7; 32:3-4; or 51, will take a very different view, and will realise that nothing can trouble the mind as sin does. As the wise physician first searches for the cause of an illness and then endeavours to take it away, so good physicians of the soul must first of all search into the cause of your sickness – your sins – and must take them away. If they do not, all their efforts are wasted. Not all the company, music, recreation, wine, diet, or worldly comforts and delights (even gaining a crown!) can comfort the distressed soul of a sinner as much as the voice of a minister who can say from God on good grounds: 'Your sins are forgiven'. But to expand what those true and good grounds are, on which a minister may safely and comfortably pronounce pardon of sins to a sinner, belongs to another context.

Notice also how, before the Lord renews the prophet's commission, or sends him to preach to the people, he first humbles him for his sins, and then, following his repentance, gives him pardon. This teaches us that no minister is well qualified for the holy duties of the ministry unless he has truly repented of his own sins, and has obtained pardon and mercy in the Messiah. Ministers work hard to gain qualifications, but the true minister of God will aim for this qualification above all others. It is the minister to whose conscience God has pronounced the pardon of his own sins who most powerfully pronounces the pardon of sins to others.

Finally, let us notice how the Lord is so concerned for Isaiah that, rather than allow him to remain uncomforted (if there was no-one to do it), an angel shall be sent to be his comforter. If there is no other prophet to do it an angel shall pronounce the pardon of his sins. Let this be an encouragement for all pastors and ministers in God's church to work hard and faithfully in their places. The goodness of the Lord will never fail them, nor shall they lack comfort whenever they stand in need of it. God will send angels from heaven to be their helpers and comforters rather than let his faithful ministers be destitute.

3. *Renewed and Recommissioned*

The third and last general point is the renewal of the prophet's commission described in Isaiah 6:8–9. It involves three things:

1. A question asked by God: 'Whom shall I send, and who will go for Us?'
2. The answer of the prophet, 'Here am I! Send me.'
3. The renewal of his commission: The Lord said, 'Go, and tell this people . . .'

The Question

The first part is a question asked by God, by way of proclamation, in which he enquires who shall go to preach to the people. 'Also I heard the voice of the Lord, saying, "Whom shall I send? and who will go for Us?"' We should not imagine that the Lord was either destitute of servants to do his will, or did not know who were able or willing to go to preach his Word. For as the apostle says about election, 'the Lord knows those who are his' (*2 Tim.* 2:19). This is all the more true when it comes to particular vocations. The Lord knows those who are his, and does not need to ask, 'Whom shall I send, or who will go?' But why then does the Lord say this? The answer is: not for his own sake, but for ours. In this way he means to instruct us in various points of sacred doctrine.

First, he shows how hard it is to find an able and godly minister. If there were not a scarcity of such men, the Lord would not have asked this question. It may be objected that there are in many Christian churches so many ministers that they cannot all be maintained, and that some are neither fully employed nor adequately provided for. This is true in every age. There were wandering Levites in the Old Testament who travelled here and there offering their services (*Judg.* 17:8; 19:18). They served for ten shekels of silver, a suit of clothes and food and drink (*Judg.* 17:10). But this disaster came on the Jewish church only when 'there was no king in Israel; everyone did what was right in his own eyes' (*Judg.* 17:6). It is a much sadder situation today if anyone travels around like this offering their services for payment since we now have kings in Israel. This is no justification for anyone to rob the church, just to please his covetous heart. But whether this is so or not (and even if it is, leaving the reformation of it to those churches and states whom it chiefly concerns) – this may be the case, and yet the Lord may complain as he does here: 'Whom shall I send?' For the Lord does not mean those who merely bear the name of Levites or priests in the Old, or of ministers in the New Testament (for there are always enough of them who, some for the sake of preferment, some for their own comfort, and some as a form of refuge, are willing to engage in such work but seek not the Lord but themselves and their own ends).

But here the Lord asks men who purely seek and undertake this task to make their priority to honour God and to gather his church, and then in all their work and ministerial duties truly to strive for the same goals: preaching God's Word as God's Word, diligently reproving, exhorting, and admonishing their people and shining before them in lives marked by good works. It is not surprising that the Lord seems here to be lighting a candle at noonday and making an open proclamation to find such a man, saying, 'Whom shall I send?' Such a man is 'one of a thousand' (*Job* 33:23). For some lack ability to discharge their duties, as Paul says, 'Who is sufficient for these things?' (*2 Cor.* 2:16). And others lack willingness to undertake the task, as God here complains, 'Who will go for Us?' What application does this have for the church today?

We may well wish that the Lord did not have as much cause today to complain because of the lack of able, faithful and godly ministers, 'Whom shall I send, And who will go for Us?' But sadly, the lack is only too apparent. It is a blemish that is too well known, and it is a work worthy of the labour of kings and princes to reform it. Is a king's evil not to be healed except by the power of a king?[1] For as long as there are only a few poor spheres of ministerial service for conscientious ministers, there will be an abundance of ministers who lack either the conscience or the ability to discharge their duties.

In the meantime, until God puts it into the hearts of governments and princes to do something about this great and necessary work, let those of us who are ministers learn our duties.[2]

First, those of us who are in the universities are here admonished to look to ourselves. Through God's blessing there are many of us and we are daily increasing in number. Let us prepare ourselves so that when God or his church says, 'Who will go for us, and whom shall I send?' many of us may be ready to be sent to the great work of the ministry. We should fear lest God will say of

---

[1] The reference is to the 'King's Evil', a form of tuberculosis which, it was believed, could be healed by the touch of the king.
[2] Here, as elsewhere, Perkins is speaking in the context of the Church of England as the nationally established Church of which the monarch was supreme governor.

us, as he did in the days of Job, that he cannot find 'one of a thousand'.

Secondly, ministers should learn from this not to content themselves merely with the name and title of ministers. They must seek to adorn the gospel. They should not take the honour and material possessions of the ministry if they will not also accept its burdens and duties. God has no need of such. Were the Lord pleased or contented with men who seek to be ministers for themselves and not for his sake, or ministers who feed themselves and not their flocks, or preach themselves and not Christ, then he would not have needed to make this proclamation. Every age has yielded its own abundant supply of such men. But let the minister who is painstaking and faithful in his service know that God and his church need him.

Finally, the Roman clergy are to be criticised here. Their number seems to be infinite; but it is lamentable how few of them are such as the Lord here seeks for. They have many orders of regular as well as secular priests. It is almost incredible how many thousands of them are Dominicans or Franciscans or are in other orders. Yet among the many millions of monks there is hardly one who in learning and other gifts is fit to be sent to the work of God. In fact their ignorance was palpably ridiculous to the world until relatively recently Luther and others in our own church made them ashamed. Since then they have made an effort (especially the Jesuits) to be well educated. It is a disgrace that despite their numbers the Lord should have cause to complain, 'Whom shall I send?' Many of the Jesuits are well educated, but as far as other qualities are concerned they are better suited to be plotters and statesmen, spies or intelligence agents, go-betweens, seducers and subverters, than to be ministers. They are better suited to be instruments of policy for evil kings than ministers of the gospel for God. But take them away, and a few selected monks (but only a few out of many thousands), and then even in terms of learning God may cry and call out in their monasteries, 'Whom shall I send?' If it is a reason for shame and misery that a church lacks those God may send, or to have only a few, then the Roman Church is shameless when it is unashamed to have so many and yet, among them all, almost none whom God may send.

In the next place, in this inquiry and question ('Whom shall I send, and who will go for Us?') the Lord teaches us that no man is to undertake this function unless God calls and sends him. This condemns the way some think that because they feel privately moved they may step forward and undertake the duties of a prophet to preach and expound Scripture. They say that these inspirations come from God's Spirit. But that is not really saying very much. For if we say that they are from the devil, or at least from their own vanity and pride, how can they disprove it? Might not Isaiah have claimed that with more reason than they? Yet he stays until God calls him. In the same way all good ministers are to wait for God's calling. If anyone asks how he will know when God calls him my response is that God ordinarily calls through his church; her voice is his. Therefore whenever the church of God says to you, 'You shall be sent, and you shall go for us,' then the Lord himself calls us to this holy task.

Thirdly, notice how the Lord says, 'Whom shall I send, and who will go for Us?' Some interpreters have used this statement, along with the third verse, where the angels sing, 'Holy, Holy, Holy', as an argument for the Trinity. But this is not substantial enough to overthrow the arguments of the Jews. A sounder and wiser judgment rests content in knowing that we have other places pregnant and plain enough to substantiate this great doctrine. It is therefore unwise to insist on this or any place which is amenable to another interpretation, in case opponents who find the argument weak judge all our proofs to be as weak. They will then persist in their blindness and do so on the basis of what we thought would have converted them. The same is true of the song of the angels in verse three, where they ascribe holiness to the Lord three times. Their repetition signifies nothing more than the continual joy and delight which the holy angels take in praising God; they can never satisfy themselves in honouring his name. The seraphim thus teach us by their example never to be weary of praising God in prayers and holy hymns, or of honouring him in our lives and callings.

But the attempt to prove the Trinity from the words 'Holy, Holy, Holy' is not based on convincing exegesis. Rather (in my opinion) we may only deduce from the words 'I' and 'us' that there are more persons in the Godhead than one. First, God the Father, or the whole deity says, 'Whom shall I send?' and then, changing the number, he says, 'Who will go for Us?' For although God may imply in the word 'us' that whoever is sent to preach is sent as much for the good of the church as for his own glory, it cannot be denied that the plural number used here and elsewhere for the deity argues a certain plurality of persons in that deity. Thus in Genesis we read that 'God said, "Let Us make man"' (*Gen.* 1:26), just as he says here, 'Who will go for Us?' Those who approve of this doctrine must grant a plurality of persons here, i.e. that there are more than one. Granted this, we can sufficiently prove from other places and by other arguments that there are actually three.

Finally, notice what God says: 'Whom shall I *send*, and who will *go* for Us?' God sends a minister to preach, and he goes for God. Note the trade and profession of a minister: he is the servant of God. So God says that he goes for him. Paul speaks similarly of himself and all other true ministers: they are 'God's fellow workers' (*1 Cor.* 3:9). On another occasion, the angel of God appeared. But it was of God, not the angel, that Paul said: 'to whom I belong and whom I serve' (*Acts* 27:23). But if any one thinks that either God speaks too favourably of such men, or Paul too partially of himself and others, let the devil himself be judge in this case. He plainly and freely confesses (although not in love either of the truth or of them): 'These men are the servants of the Most High God, who proclaim to us the way of salvation' (*Acts* 16:17). Let either God be believed, who is for them, or the devil who is against them. But what kind of servants are they? What office do they have? They are his messengers or ambassadors (*Job* 33:23); this is their profession, and their position.

Application

If ministers are God's servants, then they are not their own masters; God is their master, whose they are, for whom and from whom they come. They may not please themselves, nor serve their own pleasures, nor seek the satisfying of their own carnal lusts, either in matters of pleasure, or credit, or profit. If they do, he will call them to account since they are his servants.

Again, if they are God's servants, let them fulfil their service to God and expect their reward from God. Some ministers expect the reward and honour which is due to God's servants, but render him no service. That is unworthy of servants. Let such men remember for whom they come – from that God who, since he can give rewards, also expects service.

Men who serve diligently but are not as highly

regarded or rewarded as they deserve must learn to be content and to continue in their faithfulness, for they are God's ambassadors. Ambassadors may have gifts given to them by those to whom they are sent; but they expect their maintenance from the kings who are their own masters. The maintenance which the world should give ministers is like gifts given to ambassadors; if it comes it is no more than they deserve. But even if it does not come, faithful ministers will still do their duty and can expect their payment from their King and Master, whose they are and whom they serve.

Furthermore, if ministers are God's ambassadors, sent by him, and coming from and for him, those who either condemn or in any way injure them can be assured that as God is mighty and powerful so he will mightily revenge it. There was never a king so poor or weak but believed himself strong enough to revenge any wrong done to his ambassador. And shall God let such wickedness go unpunished? No, both they and their posterity shall suffer for it. Let Ahab (*1 Kings* 22:34), Jezebel (*2 Kings* 9:33) and Herod (*Acts* 12:23) say if this is untrue. Let all ages or histories prove the opposite if they can, that anyone who despised and abused godly ministers escaped the visible vengeance of God's revenging hands on him or his.

Again, since they are God's messengers and servants they must not be the servants of men seeking only to please, flatter or satisfy the whims of others. This is not the way for those who are God's servants. Those who are slaves to the persons, pleasures or whims of men forget that they are God's servants and have been sent by him. They must not seek to please themselves, nor to fulfil their own purposes. Rather, in every plan, whether suggested by others, or arising from their own hearts, they must immediately remind themselves: 'Who sent me here, and for whom have I come?' From and for God! They must not yield to anything, nor aim at anything, except what accords with the will and glory of him who sent them. If the great men of this world believe that it is wrong to command a servant against his will, or expect any service from him which is contrary to his own honour, then let them realise that God's ministers should not be commanded to do anything contrary to God's will or against his honour.

In addition, if ministers are God's servants, they should be concerned about their Master's glory and be ashamed to do anything, either in their doctrine or lives, which may dishonour him. Any servant who does not seek his master's credit in all his activities is unworthy of a good master.

Finally, if ministers are God's ambassadors, they must not offer their own speculations or ideas, but only the message they have received; and they must deliver it as they have received it. If they fulfil their duties faithfully, this doctrine will encourage them. They may serve with joy because they have a Master who will reward them; they may speak freely (although always with discretion) because they have a Master who will make it good. They can stand boldly in the face of their enemies since they have a Master who will defend them. And so every faithful minister may say to himself, 'I will do my duty, and deliver my message; He whom I serve, and whose I am, he who sent me and for whom I come, will deliver me.'

Isaiah's Answer

Now we must consider the prophet's answer: 'Then I said, "Here am I! Send me."' After the prophet was comforted by God, and his sins had been forgiven, he responds: 'Here am I! Send me.' First, notice the great change that has taken place. The same man who shortly before feared and shrank at the slightest appearance of God's glory, now stands forth boldly as soon as he is called and answers, 'Here am I! Send me.' This shows what a great thing it is for a minister to have his sins forgiven and to feel the favour of God towards his soul and conscience.

Here we have the answer to two great questions which are often asked.

First, many want peace of mind and conscience, but cannot get it. If they ask how they can, I give this answer: Here is the way. Do not seek it in worldly wealth, carnal pleasures, in human learning, in company, or recreations; but seek it in the favour of God and in the pardon of your sins and you cannot miss it. In this way you will have comfort in your conscience, courage before men and boldness toward God.

Secondly, many students of theology would love to be ministers, and bring honour to this calling; but they are fearful and reticent and experience an unwillingness to face the risks involved. If they ask how they can change this, I answer (or rather the example of this prophet answers for me): Let such a man place himself in God's presence, enter into himself, search his conscience, find out his sins, confess and lament them to God, seek pardon in Christ's blood, and leave them, and not rest until he hears the voice of God's Spirit sounding in his conscience telling him: 'Your sins are forgiven'. Then when God asks 'Whom shall I send?' you will answer readily and with joy, 'Here am I! Send me.'

Again, many are put off this calling when they see the contempt, the reproach and the dangers which attend it. They should notice the words of this holy prophet. When God asked, 'Whom shall I send?' he might have answered, 'Lord, I would go, but such disgrace and dis- couragement accompanies this service that I would rather be excused.' Instead, rejecting such notions, he answers decisively, 'Here am I! Send me.' What enabled him to respond like this? He was as aware of these things as any of us; he was, after all, well born and brought up, and of noble blood. It was because he saw he stood in God's favour and had him and his commission on his side. So he held on to this as sure ground on which to stand: If God is on my side, who can be against me?

Those who are hindered by discouragements have never been settled in the assurance that their sins were forgiven, nor sufficiently assured that God is on the side of all true ministers. Nor can they have been convinced that their calling has its authority from God, as is the provision, blessing, help and protection of God. This is more so of the ministry than of any other calling. If they had such settled assurance they would themselves despise the scorn, and think little of the contempt of the profane world, and with great courage and comfort set their hand to God's plough, and say with the prophet, 'Here am I! Send me.'

Secondly, let us also notice how when God asks the question the prophet does not – as he might have done – send him to others, or recommend others but offers himself: 'Here am I.' Many of us in the universities think it is enough for us to live there and send out other men, giving testimonies and letters of recommendation to other men, but never going ourselves. When the question arises, Who will go here? or Who will go to this parish? they do not say, 'Here am I!' Instead they say that either it is too small a stipend, or too great a charge, or poorly situated, or it has some other fault. Thus they refuse to be sent to it. Yet they will respond to God and to the church by suggesting another man, and give him testimonials, or commendations, and so they believe all is well. But they live too comfortably and easily to undertake willingly the contempt and burden of the ministry. When God and his church call them, such men must learn to answer with the prophet, 'Here am I! Send me.'

Theological students in the universities should pay careful attention to the prophet's answer. It is not 'I will be ready', but 'Here am I'. Why does he not take a longer time? Because he was already sufficiently qualified. Learn from this not to linger and loiter too long in speculative studies. Rather, when you are adequately furnished with learning and other qualities appropriate to your calling, show yourselves willing and ready to serve the church, whenever you are called. An apple can hang too long on the tree as well as be picked too soon. Both make it unfit for use. In a similar way many wait too long, just as others go out too soon. Both ways are unprofitable, or at least less profitable, to the church.

To conclude this second point, it is worth noting that the prophet does not say, 'Here I am', and go on his own directing. Rather he responds: 'Send me.' He wills the Lord to send him. Where are those who boast of private impulses and run when they are not sent? The prophet might have said, 'Oh, now I feel an impulse from the Spirit, therefore I will go and preach'; but he stays till he is clearly sent. Let no-one presume to press ahead in this work until he is fully resolved in his conscience that God and his church have said to him, 'Go'.

Although a man is well and sufficiently qualified, let him sit still and await God's timing and then let him say, 'Here am I! Send me'. Let him rest content until he is sent. If anyone says it is inappropriate for a man to say this of himself, my reply is that he should say so not in words, but in deeds. Let him prove himself and give the church evidence of his gifts. Then, if he is found to be qualified his practice is consistent with and means much more than if he had said, 'Here I am, send me.'

In this way we see that the prophet refused to stir until he was sent. Consequently in the next statement he is commanded to go. 'And he said, "Go, and tell this people . . .".

Isaiah's Commission

Here is the third and last point: the essential words of his commission. Here (after God had asked for someone to go, and the prophet had presented himself and offered his services) God gives him leave to go and further equips him with authority, both to go and to speak.

The principal point here is that the authority of the prophet's calling is derived from God himself in plain and clear terms: 'Go, and speak'. Until then the prophet did not go. Similarly, in the New Testament, the apostles did not go into the world to preach until they had received their commission, 'Go therefore and make disciples of all the nations' (*Matt.* 28:19). Following them, Paul did not preach until he was told, 'Arise and go' (*Acts* 9:6).

In all of this the pride and presumption of those who dare to go on their own authority and will not stay until the Lord says to them, 'Go, and speak', stand revealed and condemned. Those men are bolder than either the extraordinary prophets of the Old Testament, or the apostles who are the extraordinary ministers of the New. Those men always had their warrant with them when they went. If anyone asks why it is necessary they should have this, the reasons are many.

First, prophets and ministers are God's deputies and commissioners. It is only right that they should have authority from their Lord and Master. Secondly, neither their words nor their deeds are creditable nor do they have any power in them unless they are spoken on the basis of a commission. Nor do their labours enjoy any blessing unless God gives it. Thirdly, they have no promise of protection or safety unless they are God's ambassadors. And how can they be so, unless they are called and sent by God, and have authority given to them by him? For these reasons no-one is to thrust himself into the ministry without a call from God. No wonder then if those men who choose and call themselves and run when they are not sent are subject to all dangers. They are outside God's protection, and their labours are without profit because no blessing or promise of God was given to them. God may justly say to them, 'Let him that sent you protect you; let him that sent you bless your labours.'

It will then be asked, How may I know if God is commanding me go? For God does not speak now from heaven as he did to this prophet. True, we are to look for no such visions or apparitions from heaven, for ordinarily there are none, and the Roman Catholic Church deceives itself and cheats the world when it tells us of apparitions which its monks and friars experienced. For now God ordinarily speaks in a different way to his church. In general duties God speaks to us out of his Word, the Holy Scriptures while in particular and personal duties (in matters which the Word does not directly address), he speaks to the individual through his own conscience and the voice of his church.

God's Word shows us the dignity and excellency of the calling to be a minister of the Word (*1 Cor.* 4:1). Such are his messengers and ambassadors and he wants them to love and use it. The necessity of his Word lies in the fact that it teaches the way to salvation; ordinarily God's church is not gathered, nor are men's souls saved, without it. This may stir you up to undertake the burden.

But this is a general consideration. How can you know

for yourself whether God wants you to go or not? You must ask both your own conscience and the church. For if you are genuinely willing, and are fully and worthily qualified, then God bids you to go. Your conscience must judge of your willingness and the church of your ability. Just as you may not trust other men to judge your inclination or affection, so you may not trust your own judgment to judge your worthiness or adequacy. If therefore your own conscience tells you, after careful self-examination, that you do not love and desire this calling above any other, then God is not sending you. If this is true of you it is not God but some worldly and sinister consideration that has motivated you and put you forward.

But even if you desire the call to the ministry, if the church of God does not recognise your sufficiency, God is not sending you. But if, on the contrary, your conscience truly testifies that you desire to serve God and his church in this calling above any other; *and* if, when you have indicated this to the church and your gifts and learning have been tested, the church (that is, many who are learned, wise, and godly and those whom the church has publicly appointed for that purpose) approves of your desire and of your ability to serve God in his ministry, *and* if the church issues a public call and bids you go, then God himself has bid you to go. That is as effectual a calling as if you had heard the voice of God from heaven. As in repentance, so it is here. If your conscience tells you that you have truly repented, and if you can make that known to the church with clear evidence so that a minister of God can pronounce the pardon of your sins to you; if you rest in this, and know it is effectual, as if God had told you himself, then your sins are pardoned. If you have the testimony of your own conscience and then of the church, you can rest in that as in the voice of

God. This is the kind of calling for which we are to look in these days.

This doctrine justly condemns the presumption of those who act on the basis of private impulses and from carnal motivations. They are justly left without blessing or protection. But on the other side, some do great wrong to God and his church. They cannot deny, but actually acknowledge the ministry to be the highest calling; their gifts are approved by the church of God; yet they will not believe the testimony of the church. Rather they accept their own private judgments, which in this case are no competent judge, either for or against. Let such men know that they are actually opposing God himself. For it is certain that when the inward calling of the conscience and the outward calling of the church concur God himself calls and bids us, 'Go, and speak'.

Finally, let us note the authority with which a minister of God comes to us, and fulfils his function. It is the immediate authority and commission of God. By it he is bidden, 'Go, and speak'. If this is the case, the world should be persuaded to fear to do any wrong, either to that calling or to those who come with such a commission from God himself. But if the secular world is not persuaded, at least let this be a comfort and encouragement to all true ministers: if God bids them go, he himself will go with them. If he sends them, he will not forsake them, but assist them and bless them and open their mouths and enlarge their hearts and harden their foreheads, and empower their words to convert his children and to confound and astound the hearts of his enemies. If he sends them he will defend and protect them, so that not even one of their hairs is able to perish. If he sends them he will provide for them and reward them adequately. He will honour them in the hearts of his own people and magnify them in the faces of their enemies. And lastly, if he sends them he will pay their wages: an eternal weight of comfort here and of glory in heaven. Just as they are here bidden to go, so then they will be bidden to come. And that will not only be with the general call of all the elect – 'Come, you blessed of My Father, inherit the kingdom prepared for you' (*Matt.* 25:34); but with a particular call which belongs to those who are faithful in this service: 'Well done, good and faithful servant, Enter into the joy of your lord' (*Matt.* 25:21).

> *Blessed is he who comes in the name of the Lord.*
> *(Psa.* 118:26)

> *Those who are wise shall shine,*
> *Like the brightness of the firmament,*
> *And those who turn many to righteousness*
> *Like the stars for ever and ever.*
> *(Dan.* 12:3)

> *Let a man so consider us, as servants of Christ*
> *and stewards of the mysteries of God.*
> *(1 Cor.* 4:1)